Multicultural Sing and Learn

Folk Songs and Monthly Activities

by
Carolyn Meyer
and
Kel Pickens

illustrated by Tom Foster

Cover by Tom Foster

Copyright © 1994, Good Apple

ISBN No. 0-86653-830-5

Printing No. 987654321

Good Apple
1204 Buchanan St., Box 299
Carthage, IL 62321-0299

Paramount Publishing

Introduction

The classrooms of today consist of a mixture of many cultures. Each is valuable and has much to offer. In this book we used the original versions of folk songs from various cultures. These are followed by new words to the old tunes that explain or introduce a concept. Many of the children in the classroom will immediately know the original songs. When the words are changed to relate new information, it should build their positive self-concept and make their culture an important part of the ongoing learning process. Children who are not members of these particular cultures will absorb information about other cultures and learn to value them as sources of new information. The exercises and activity sheets following each song tie in with the new lyrics to further the learning process. The overall result of using this book is that children will understand that learning can happen by using information from a variety of cultures.

NOTE: Many of these original folk songs have strong religious backgrounds. Please take this into consideration while reviewing each section for your curriculum. You may want to send notes home to parents or guardians on this subject.

Table of Contents

This book is lovingly dedicated to those who sat with us all during the writing of it: B.C., Jade, Kyotee, Rapport, and Yella Fella.

To order a cassette tape containing all of the songs printed in this book, sung by Carolyn Meyer (original versions only), send $11.00 in United States currency only to:
Multicultural Sing and Learn Cassette
Giant Blueberry Music
115 Melrose Drive
Stillwater, OK 74074
(405) 377-9278 No credit card orders please!
(Make your check payable to Giant Blueberry Music.)

GA1522

August

1

GA1522

My Farm
Argentine Folk Song

Come now and see my farm, for it is beau - ti - ful,

Come now and see my farm, for it is beau - ti - ful. El pol - li - to sounds like (Chicken)

this: peep, peep; El pol - li - to sounds like this: peep, peep; Oh

pas, ca - ma - rade, oh pas, ca - ma - rade, oh pas, oh pas, oh pas, oh

pas, ca - ma - rade, oh pas, ca - ma - rade, oh pas, oh, pas, oh pas.

GA1522

More Animals for "My Farm":

2. El patito (duck) sounds like this: quack, quack.
3. El chanchito (pig) sounds like this: oink, oink.
4. El gatito (kitten) sounds like this: meow, meow.
5. El perrito (puppy) sounds like this: bow-wow.
6. El burrito (burro) sounds like this: hee-haw.

"My Friend" sung to the tune of "My Farm"
Come now and make new friends for it's the first of school,
Come now and make new friends for it's the first of school.
My new friend's name is this:_____(fill in name)
My new friend's name is this:_____(fill in another name)
Oh pas, camarade, Oh pas, camarade, Oh pas, Oh pas, Oh pas,
Oh pas, camarade, Oh pas, camarade, Oh pas, Oh pas, Oh pas.
(Pas, camarade means "Come, friend.")

New Friends

Children are paired up (partners) and in a big circle for this activity. Everyone may choose a partner or the teacher may pair them up. Partners will ask each other their first names. Each child will introduce his or her partner on the line of the song that has a blank space left for the name after learning the new version of the song. The teacher will designate which person will introduce his or her partner first, and then the game will continue around the circle until everyone has been introduced. The teacher may wish to occasionally point to who's next if the children get mixed up. Only two children (one set of partners) may be introduced each time the song is sung. Therefore, if there are twenty children in your class, you'll need to sing the song ten times. To avoid repeating the whole song so many times, just repeat the two lines, "My new friend's name is this:_____; My new friend's name is this:_____."

Any names can be fitted into the blank space by adjusting the rhythm. During the refrain that's in Spanish (Oh pas, camarade) have each child shake his or her new friend's hand. A variation on the refrain that you may wish to try is to have the children cross their arms in front of themselves to link up and shake the hands of the children on both sides of them in the circle. Special note: If a child has a one syllable name like Ben, have the other child who's introducing him say, "He's Ben!" in the blank space.

What Is a Friend?

This exercise will help children discern what constitutes friendly behavior as opposed to unfriendly behavior. Many children really don't know what actions or behaviors may be considered as unfriendly until they are pointed out to them. The teacher will give each child a red and a green piece of construction paper. Children in grades three through five should copy the word *friendly* onto the green paper and the word *unfriendly* onto the red paper. The teacher should already have these words printed on the paper for children in grades k through two. Then the teacher will instruct the children to listen to each example of behavior and decide if the behavior is friendly or unfriendly. If the behavior described is friendly, the children will hold up their green papers. If the behavior is unfriendly, the children are to hold up the red papers. Remind the younger children that red and green also mean stop and go. We all want to stop unfriendly behavior and go with friendly behavior! Discuss each answer given before going on to the next example so that anyone who held up the wrong colored paper understands why others' answers were different.

Examples:

1. One child hits another child on the head. (red, unfriendly)
2. After singing a song as a class, a child raises his or her hand and says for everyone to hear that another child's singing is "terrible!" and that he or she wants to move to another seat. (red, unfriendly)
3. A child drops the green paper on the floor and another child picks it up and returns it. (green, friendly)
4. One child is speaking when all of a sudden another child interrupts. (red, unfriendly)
5. A child compliments another on how nice he or she looks. (green, friendly)
6. One child laughs at another's answer. (red, unfriendly)
7. A child refuses to sit by a certain other child. (red, unfriendly)
8. One child loans another child his or her crayons. (green, friendly)
9. One child cuts in line in front of another child. (red, unfriendly)
10. A child holds the door open for another child who's coming in. (green, friendly)

Add your own examples to these so that they fit your own class.

GA1522

Anton Firulero
Costa Rican Folk Song

Lively

An - ton, An - ton, An - ton Fi - ru - le - ro, Each one, each

one will play his own way, oh, And the one, and the one who does - n't o -

bey, oh, Must do, must do, what An - ton, what An - ton will say, oh.

"Same but Different" sung to the tune of "Anton Firulero"

We're all the same and yet we're so diff'rent!
We all need love and we want to give it!
Yet we each have a life unlike any other,
And talents we can share with, can share with each other!

5

GA1522

Teaching with Totem Poles

Certain Native Americans of the northwestern coast of North America erected a post carved and painted with a series of symbols before a dwelling. These symbols quite often represented an animal, plant, natural object, or god that told a story of an ancestral relationship.

This activity will actively involve children in discovering that there is strength through diversity. They will discover that with their self-portraits they may look different from one another; but by being required to form a unit (tribe) to accomplish tasks, they may learn that the contributions of each individual are important.

The teacher should provide one long piece of white butcher paper about six feet long (1.85 meters) for every four to six students in the class. In a class of twenty-four students you can have either four to six paper totem poles made with butcher paper. The teacher will cut each paper into four, five, or six sections using various cut patterns. The top and bottom of each paper should have straight edges as well as the sides. But any sections from the middle should have patterns on the tops and bottoms unlike any other cuts. Eventually these pieces will fit back together like a puzzle to form the original sheet of butcher paper for each tribe.

Once all sheets have been cut in this fashion, mix the pieces together and distribute them to the class members randomly. Instruct the children to use crayons, colored pencils, or whatever they like to draw a self-portrait on the piece of butcher paper they've been given. Have each child write his or her name on the back in one corner. When everyone has finished, have the children with a straight edge at the top come to the front of the classroom and hold their self-portraits up. These are, of course, the tops of each totem pole. Now have the remaining children come to the front of the classroom and in single file see if their self-portraits fit with the next piece in each totem pole. If their pieces fit the teacher applies tape to the back side to begin forming the poles. If a child's piece does not fit, he or she can go to the rear of the line and try again and keep trying until the piece fits into one of the poles. Each pole will be finished when the bottom piece with a straight edge completes the pole. Since top and bottom pieces both have straight edges, prevent a mix-up from occurring by labeling the bottom of each piece with a small *B* in pencil. Be sure to label all pieces of the totem pole with a small *B* so that students will know which side to draw their self-portraits on and avoid drawing their pictures upside down. Tell them that it is extremely important that they draw their self-portraits on the side labeled with the *B* and the *B* stands for the bottom of the paper. Tell them that the reason they must do this correctly is so that their puzzle pieces will fit together correctly later to form their totem poles. Have the children get into groups (tribes) around their own

totem poles. Each child should think of a talent or ability that he or she has. If children are having a difficult time thinking of a talent or ability, help them by telling them that a talent can be nearly anything that they do well. Once all children have thought of talents or abilities, they should give themselves tribal names that reflect the talents or abilities. Then they need to think of stories about their totem poles. The stories need to deal with how they became a tribe, and they may be as fantastic and imaginative as the children would like to make them. It should also involve their talents or abilities. At this point, they may want to add to their own self-portraits on the totem poles to go along with the stories of their tribes and to reflect their talents or abilities. Once they've thought of their stories, they'll have to agree on a name within their groups. Here is a sample story about a tribe named Weshareit:

"Many years ago, when there were no vehicles around but bicycles, the Weshare-it Tribe was formed. It began when Fix-It-Up Carlos had no bicycle. Singing Mary and her friend, Green Thumb Bobby, each had bicycles that were made of yellow daffodils. One morning they were racing each other across the land where Fix-It-Up Carlos dwelled. They were unaware that coming in the opposite direction, racing on bicycles made of bird feathers, were Artistic Lisa and Peaceful Bill. Fix-It-Up Carlos was barely able to dive out of the way before everyone crashed head-on, resulting in a large shower of feathers and daffodils. The four bicyclists weren't hurt, but unfortunately, all that remained of their wonderful bicycles was still raining down in a shower all around. And it all fell right into the lake. A huge quarrel erupted with everyone blaming the others for the wreck. Peaceful Bill stepped in immediately and stopped the quarrel. But soon they began shedding tears over the loss of their beautiful bicycles. Fix-It-Up Carlos was wise enough to gather their tears in a bottle which quickly filled to the brim. Green Thumb Bobby just happened to have some daffodil bulbs which he planted. After he'd watered them with the children's tears, Singing Mary began to sing. Her singing was so beautiful that the birds flew around her head and gave her many of their feathers. Her sweet singing made the daffodils sprout and grow right away. Then Artistic Lisa and Fix-It-Up Carlos gathered the feathers and daffodils and constructed four new bicycles. The children were delighted with their new bikes. They quickly pointed out that there were enough flowers and feathers left over for them to build one more bicycle. They all helped in the building of this one and then gladly gave it to Fix-It-Up Carlos. All five rode together across many lands and they called themselves the Weshareit Tribe which means 'from sharing comes more.'"

GA1522

If this mythical story were applied to the totem pole of self-portraits, the children could add the following embellishments to their self-portraits:

Fix-It-Up Carlos	hammer or other tools
Singing Mary	music notes or treble clef sign
Green Thumb Bobby	flowers, vines, thumbs
Artistic Lisa	paintbrush
Peaceful Bill	peace sign, dove, olive branch

Once each tribe is satisfied with the way their totem pole looks and with their story, they should share it with the rest of the class/other tribes. They may either write it down and read it or just tell it to the other tribes. There are many ways to share a story. One of the tribe members could read the narration while the others act it out. They might read it all together like a choral reading. They might each read a part of the story. They might write it in a poem or write new words to a familiar tune and sing it. For children who are too young to write, they should either tell their stories to the teacher who writes them down or have some older students write their stories down as they tell them.

The next song is a Native American ceremonial anthem. The Zuni Indians honor the sun and live mostly in Arizona and New Mexico. In a ceremony at the rising of the sun, the whole tribe comes to greet the sun and ask for strength and guidance.

8

Zuni Sunrise Song
Zuni Indians

Here is an alternative verse for the "Zuni Sunrise Song." This verse deals with sharing.

When we try to share, (Echo) When we try to share,
We also learn to cooperate, help others out, and communicate.
Giving of ourselves builds community,
Making of our school one big family.
When we try to share, (Echo) When we try to share.

9

GA1522

The Sharing Chain Reaction

This activity will demonstrate to children in kindergarten through second grade that by sharing what they have with others they can accomplish much more than by remaining solitary. The teacher should divide the class into three small groups with approximately the same number of children in each group. Give one group of children small bottles of glue (one per child); give another group scissors (one per child); and give the last group various colors of construction paper (one per child). He or she then needs to tell all of the children that they are to construct a chain using only what they've just been handed. Initially there may be some confusion and questions from the children about how this is to be done. The teacher should be patient but not answer directly. If no one catches on after about five minutes, the teacher may wish to give the clue that the children are allowed to work with other people in the room and share what they have. That should spark cooperation among threesomes with each one possessing either paper, scissors, or glue. And they should all be able to construct a chain by working together. The teacher may also suggest putting their chains with other groups' chains to make even larger chains to hang up around the room or in the hallway. If by chance some children are able to construct a chain without cooperating with others, their inventions should be incorporated into the chains right along with those groups who did cooperate and work together. After all the chains have been finished and hung up, the teacher should discuss with the children the following things:

1. Did they enjoy working with others?
2. Would it have been possible to make a chain with just glue?
3. Would it have been possible to make a chain with just scissors?
4. Would your chains have looked as nice if you hadn't had glue or scissors?
5. Does sharing make things easier?
6. Is it fun to share?

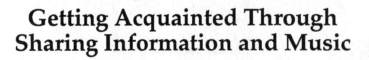

Getting Acquainted Through Sharing Information and Music

This is an activity for third through fifth graders. This needs some planning ahead of time, or it could be done on a regular day each week for several weeks until everyone gets a chance to do the activity. It could be done for a certain time period each day and spread out over a week. The teacher should designate several students to bring a cassette tape that they like to listen to on a certain day. They will be allowed to play one selection from their tape on that day. Remind them not to bring tapes with offensive language on them. Give them the option to bring a record or a compact disc. If a child doesn't have any kind of music selection to bring of his or her own, have that student get one from the library.

GA1522

Of course, the teacher needs to have a cassette tape player, record player, and/or compact disc player on hand to use when playing the children's musical selections. Before a student talks about what song is going to be played and who performs it, the teacher requests that he or she first share information about him- or herself with the rest of the class. However, rather than just telling facts, a game of sharing information is possible. Tell the student to give three "facts" about him- or herself. One fact is true; the other two are not. The class will listen and decide which is the true fact about the person. If they guess it right the first try, then the student will go on to play his or her selection of music. Let the person telling the three facts call on people to guess which fact is true. Tolerance for other people's choices of music should be encouraged by the teacher. Tell the children that music is a matter of personal taste.

Banuwa
Folk Song from Liberia

Ba - nu - wa, ba - nu - wa, ba - nu - wa yo.————— Ba - nu - wa,

ba - nu - wa, ba - nu - wa yo.———— A - la - no, neh—— ni a

la no; a la no, neh—— ni a la no. Neh ni a la

no; Neh ni a la no. Neh ni a la no;

Neh ni a la no. Ba - nu- wa, ba - nu- wa, ba - nu- wa yo.—————

Here is an alternative set of words to be sung to the tune of "Banuwa." They deal with good hygiene and health.

Keep Yourself Clean

Take a bath when you can; keep yourself clean. (Repeat.)
Once a day is okay; make your skin gleam! (Repeat.)
A shower is so refreshing; a shower is so refreshing. (Repeat.)
Dry off thoroughly; dry off thoroughly. (Repeat.)
Then put on clean clothes; then put on clean clothes. (Repeat.)
When you're fresh, when you're clean, people will know. (Repeat.)

GA1522

Putting Together Good Health and Hygiene Habits

Children in grades k through two will be able to learn about good health and hygiene by using the puzzle pieces provided on the next two pages. The teacher needs to copy enough of each page for every child to have a copy. Once children have their pages, they're to cut out each animal picture around the dotted lines. When they've cut out all ten of the animals, give each child the next page which has the ten hygiene/health concepts listed on the bottom halves of ten different shapes. Instruct them to place the animal picture shape that matches the top half of each of the ten forms on the page. Once the teacher has checked to see where a child has put the shapes and finds them correct, that child can paste them on the paper. After everything has been pasted in correctly, the teacher should begin the discussion by asking the following questions:

1. What is this animal?
2. What's the animal doing?
3. Is this something we can do too?
4. How often should we do it?
5. Read the concept from the bottom part of the forms to children who are too young to read. Children who are older may be able to read it for themselves.

Third graders through fifth graders could match up these ten concepts with animals too easily. Therefore, the teacher may desire to hand out only the first sheet with the depictions of the animals on them and not the second forms sheets. Let them come up with what health/hygiene concept each picture is depicting. You may wish to write these on the board as they go through the animals. After all ten are written on the board, have them each pick a concept that they would like to illustrate on their own health/hygiene poster. Encourage them to be creative, using their own ideas whether it's with animals, people, or objects. The pictures in the book may serve as a guide and springboard for them to generate their own ideas. No words are allowed on the posters! Display the finished posters in the classroom and then see if the rest of the class can figure out what concept has been portrayed. After all have been guessed correctly, words might be added as an option. These could be displayed in the hallway instead of just in the classroom. They could be shared with other classes of younger children also.

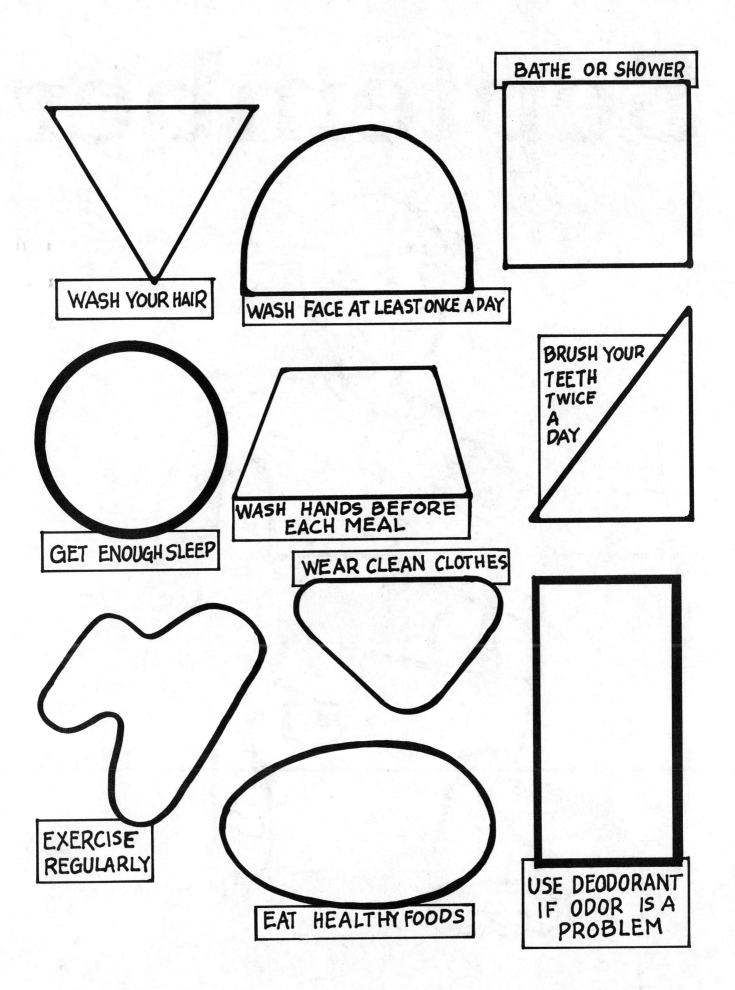

WASH YOUR HAIR

WASH FACE AT LEAST ONCE A DAY

BATHE OR SHOWER

GET ENOUGH SLEEP

WASH HANDS BEFORE EACH MEAL

BRUSH YOUR TEETH TWICE A DAY

WEAR CLEAN CLOTHES

EXERCISE REGULARLY

EAT HEALTHY FOODS

USE DEODORANT IF ODOR IS A PROBLEM

September

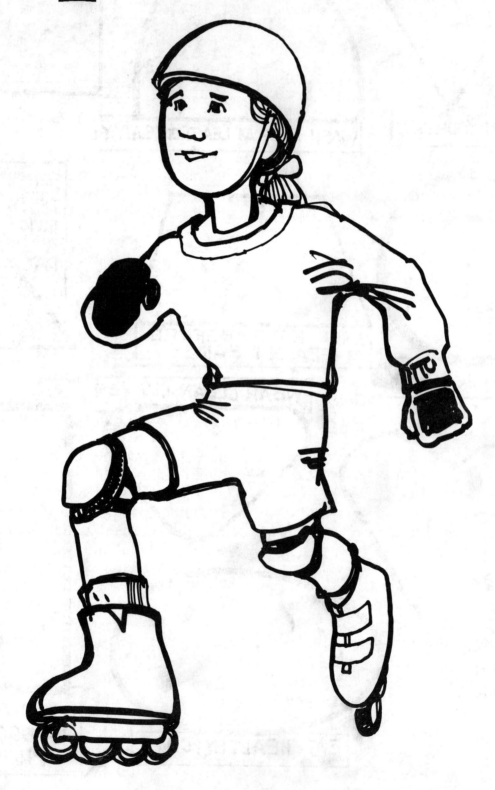

16

Li'l Liza Jane
African-American Folk Song

I've a gal and you have none, Li'l Li - za Jane! I've a gal and you have none,

Li`l Li - za Jane! Oh! E - li - za, Li`l Li - za Jane! Oh! E - li - za, Li`l Li - za Jane!

Here is an alternative verse to "Li'l Liza Jane" that your students might enjoy singing. Be sure to tell them that quite often, folk songs have many different versions since most of them were passed down by one person singing them to another. They were usually passed down orally from one generation to the next.

I've got a house in Baltimore, Li'l Liza Jane.
Streetcar runs right by my door, Li'l Liza Jane.
Oh, Eliza, Li'l Liza Jane.
Oh, Eliza, Li'l Liza Jane.

Math with Li'l Liza Jane!

Next, use the tune of "Li'l Liza Jane" to teach some math facts that are appropriate to your particular grade level. The tune may be used with very easy addition. For example:

> Two plus three is five, I know! Li'l Liza Jane!
> Two plus four is six, I know! Li'l Liza Jane!
> Oh, Eliza, Li'l Liza Jane! Oh, Eliza, Li'l Liza Jane!

You may have the children sing any combinations of numbers that will work with what your class is studying. It will work with subtraction. For example:

> Three from five is two, I know! Li'l Liza Jane!
> Five from six is one, I know! Li'l Liza Jane!

Likewise, tailor your examples for the class to sing to what they are studying and capable of handling. This song would also work quite well with the multiplication tables. For example:

> Two times three is six, I know! Li'l Liza Jane!
> Three times four is twelve, I know! Li'l Liza Jane!

For more difficult multiplication tables, change the words to:

> Seven times eight is fifty-six, Li'l Liza Jane!
> Nine times nine is eighty-one, Li'l Liza Jane!

You might have the children start with the twos and go all the way through them before they sing the Refrain of "Oh, Eliza, Li'l Liza Jane." Then go onto the threes, fours, etc. Make the verses as difficult as your students can handle.

GA1522

Measure Math

A measure in this song is 2 beats long since the time signature is $\frac{2}{4}$. You can tell where one measure begins and ends by looking for the bar lines. | |
Here's a math problem that your students can solve by multiplying.

> This song, "Li'l Liza Jane," is 16 measures long. If we got very excited one day and sang this song 5 times, how many measures would we have sung? Have them multiply 16 times 5.

Change the number of times sung so that your students will have the experience of multiplying.

Here's an example for a subtraction problem using the measures in the song.

> One day we were singing the song, "Li'l Liza Jane," which is 16 measures long. All of a sudden, the fire alarm sounded and we had to leave . We were right in the seventh measure of the song when we rushed out! How many more measures would we have to sing to finish the song?

Change the numbers in the above example to give your students the opportunity to subtract more.

An upper level division exercise would be:

> If we sang 48 measures and the song is only 16 measures long, how many times would we have sung the song?

This will give your students a chance to divide. Be sure to change the numbers to give them lots of practice.

Here's an example of an addition problem for you to build on:

> We loved singing and moving with the song "Li'l Liza Jane" so much that we decided to add some verses onto the song. If we added three measures onto the sixteen that are already there, how many would we have?

Gear this exercise to the level of your students.

For very young students, you may wish them to count just the number of beats in the whole song (32: 2 beats per measure, 16 measures). They might count how many times "Liza Jane" is sung (4). There are any number of math opportunities by using "Li'l Liza Jane."

Li'l Liza Jane Rap

Allow the class to make up a rap about "Li'l Liza Jane." Ask them the question, "Who is Li'l Liza Jane?" They will then compose a rap piece to tell you the answer. It may be better to divide your class into small groups of about four or five children for this activity. The raps will have no specific number of measures. When the children perform the raps, each group will do theirs without stopping between groups.

GA1522

If the children have trouble keeping the beat going between different groups, go ahead and let one group perform and take a complete stop between them and the next group. When performing, one or two people in the group could say the words of the rap that they've composed while the other three or four make body or mouth sounds that keep the rap beat (steady beat) going. Not everyone in the group would have to make sounds; one person might want to do a dance as the rap is spoken.

Of Cultural Note

Make the students aware of this information. The music of African-Americans is different from other forms of American music due to the history of slavery. The slaves were restricted in what kind of music they were allowed to perform by their masters. Therefore, this caused them to combine their African music with the music they heard that was done by their masters.

One of the most outstanding characteristics of African-American music is its rhythm. It makes most people want to move in some way when they hear it. When we sing, create percussive body sounds (like in the rap), move, or dance, we are experiencing African-American music in the way it might have originally been intended to be experienced.

One Day My Mother Went to the Market
Italian Folk Song

19

GA1522

More verses for "One Day My Mother Went to the Market"

2. One day my mother went to the market and she bought a little pig.
A pig? A pig! But when my mother started to cook him,
He got up and danced a jig. A jig? A jig!
Oh, he said, "Oink, oink, oink, though I'd like to stay;
Though I'd like to stay,"
Oh, he said, "Oink, oink, oink, and he ran away;
And he ran away!

3. One day my mother went to the market and she bought a pretty lamb.
A lamb? A lamb! But when my mother started to cook him,
He said, "Who do you think I am?" I am? I am!
Oh, he said, "Baa, baa, baa. I'm silly, it's true;
I'm silly, it's true!" Oh, he said, "Baa, baa, baa.
Not as silly as you; not as silly as you."

4. One day my mother went to the market and she bought a lovely hen.
A hen? A hen! But when my mother started to cook her
She began to cluck again. Again? Again!
Oh, she said, "Cluck, cluck, cluck, cluck, cluck,"
But she forgot; but she forgot.
Oh, she said, "Cluck, cluck, cluck, cluck, cluck,"
And fell into the pot, and fell into the pot.

Here are three new verses to the tune of "One Day My Mother Went to the Market." These are about different sports and scoring differences. They will lead into some math and language arts activities.

1. One day my brother was playing baseball and he hit the
winning home run! A home run? A home run!
But when he ran and touched each base then I thought he
had a point for each one. For each one? For each one!
He scored one run touching home plate;
The score will stay low at that rate.
He scored one run touching home plate,
But a home run's great! But a home run's great!

20

GA1522

2. Basketball is a game that my sister loves and she is
   good at shooting. At shooting? At shooting!
   She dribbles down the basketball court and shoots a
   basket while I'm rooting. You're rooting? I'm rooting!
   She gets 2 points for every score from certain places
   on the floor. She gets 2 points for every score
   Or sometimes 3 which is even more!

3. One night my cousin was playing football and he scored
   his team a touchdown! A touchdown? A touchdown!
   But when the kicker booted the extra point he acted
   like a big clown! A big clown? A big clown!
   The score was now 7 to none, although the game had
   just begun. The score was now 7 to none;
   They had scored 6 points on my cousin's run!

Team Members Count

Count the number of team members in each picture. Cut out the different balls. Match the correct ball with the correct sport, but make sure that the number on that ball matches the number of players in that team picture. Paste the ball in the right place on the picture.

GA1522

Concession Stand Math

Sporting events quite often have a concession stand selling various food items to the spectators. Copy a page of "Sales Tickets" for each child in the class and have children cut them into individual squares. Then combine all of the squares into a big box that children will draw from later. For each child make a copy of the "Concession Stand Math" work sheet picturing the different food items. Tell children to pretend they are the managers of their own concession stands at a sporting event. Children are to work alone with this sheet, pricing each item according to how much they would be willing to pay. Tell them that nothing is to be priced over $2.00. Once they have priced their items, let each child draw 10 tickets from the "Sales Tickets" box. These 10 tickets represent their sales for the day. According to how they priced their items, they will add up their total sales for the day. The teacher may need to demonstrate on the board how to add these items. One method is to add the individual sale item prices to get a sum for that sale.

(For instance: the sales ticket drawn says, "3 popcorns" and the child has priced popcorn for 50¢ each. So add 50¢ + 50¢ + 50¢ = $1.50.)

Each child will have a total of 10 sums for the day's sales. Those sums can then be added together to get a daily total for that day's sales. Of course, other methods can be employed to acquire these daily totals. One such method is a running total which is achieved by taking the sums of each individual sale and continuously adding them to a running total sum until all 10 sales have been added.

(For instance: Child draws a sales ticket that says, "2 sodas" and has priced soda at 50¢ each. Add 50¢ + 50¢ = $1.00. Next sales ticket says, "1 cotton candy" and child has priced it at 75¢ so add $1.00 + 75¢ = $1.75. Next sales ticket says, "1 hot dog" and child has priced hot dogs at $1.00 each, so add $1.75 + $1.00 = $2.75.)

If the children are able to multiply, you may wish to have them figure products on each sale by multiplying the number of items sold by their price per item.
(Sales ticket says, "4 sodas" and sodas are priced at 50¢ each, so 4 x 50¢ = $2.00.)

Then they could add the products together to get the daily total. Play this game for 5 days in a row. Then add all 5 Daily Total Sale amounts to get the Grand Total Sales for the week. If you wish, have the students divide their Grand Total Sales by 5 to find the average daily sales.

GA1522

Sales Tickets

3 popcorns	2 sodas	1 cotton candy	2 candy bars	4 hot dogs	2 peanuts	2 popcorns	5 sodas
3 cotton candy	1 candy bar	2 hot dogs	4 peanuts	1 popcorn	5 sodas	1 cotton candy	3 candy bars
2 hot dogs	3 peanuts	6 popcorns	1 soda	2 cotton candy	6 candy bars	4 hot dogs	5 peanuts
5 popcorns	3 sodas	4 cotton candy	3 candy bars	6 hot dogs	3 peanuts	7 popcorns	5 sodas
1 cotton candy	2 candy bars	3 hot dogs	4 peanuts	5 popcorns	1 soda	2 cotton candy	3 candy bars
3 hot dogs	2 peanuts	1 popcorn	2 sodas	3 cotton candy	4 candy bars	5 hot dogs	6 peanuts
6 popcorns	5 sodas	4 cotton candy	3 candy bars	2 hot dogs	1 peanuts	1 popcorn	2 sodas
3 cotton candy	4 candy bars	5 hot dogs	6 peanuts	5 popcorns	4 sodas	3 cotton candy	4 candy bars
3 hot dogs	2 peanuts	1 popcorn	2 sodas	3 cotton candy	4 candy bars	5 hot dogs	6 peanuts

Concession Stand Math (Work Sheet)

Popcorn

_____
Price

Soda

_____
Price

Cotton Candy

_____
Price

Candy Bars

_____
Price

Hot Dog

_____
Price

Peanuts

_____
Price

Daily Total Sales

Day 1: _____

Day 2: _____

Day 3: _____

Day 4: _____

Day 5: _____

Grand Total Sales

_____

GA1522

In Bahia Town
Brazilian Folk Song

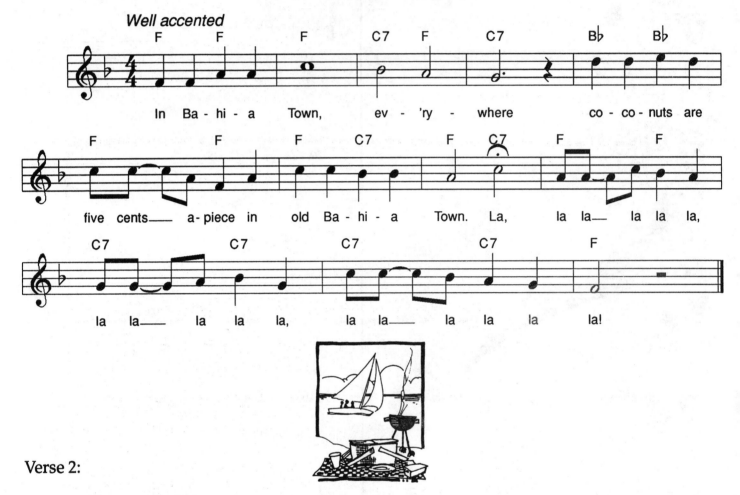

Well accented

In Ba - hi - a Town, ev - 'ry - where co - co - nuts are

five cents___ a - piece in old Ba - hi - a Town. La,

la la___ la la la, la la___ la la la la!

Verse 2:

In Bahia town, ev'rywhere, vatapa* is five cents a plate in old Bahia town.
La, la la la la la, la la la la la, la la la la la la.

*Vatapa is a national dish of Brazil.

Alternate verses sung to the tune of "In Bahia Town"

Labor Day

When we celebrate Labor Day ev'ryone should rest and relax,
And not work on this date. La . . .

Labor Day is when some countries honor people who work so hard,
And signals summer's end. La . . .

For the students' information: Labor Day is celebrated on the first Monday in September in the United States, Puerto Rico, and Canada. It's a day of rest and recreation and signifies the end of summer. It also commemorates the successful struggle for a shorter working day of eight hours. In Europe, Labor Day is celebrated on May 1.

GA1522

Labor Day Dates

Here is an activity for younger children. Have them arrange the three dates in the correct order. Tell them what happened on each date.

1887: Oregon became the first state to make Labor Day a legal holiday.

1894: Grover Cleveland signed a bill making Labor Day a national holiday.

1882: In September the first Labor Day parade took place in New York City.

Leisure Time Pantomime

Since Labor Day is a time for rest and recreation, many people use their leisure time in differing ways. To illustrate these different types of leisure time activities, have students pantomime their own leisure time activities. You may wish to divide the class up into two teams. Team members will pantomime their favorite leisure time activity for their own teammates to guess. Set a time limit of one to two minutes. If they guess correctly before time runs out, their team gets a point. If they fail to guess the answer when time runs out, the other team may make one guess and steal the point if they're correct. Continue alternating teams and playing until everyone has had a turn to pantomime. You may wish to make a rule that television viewing is off-limits as a leisure time activity. No activity may be used more than once. This will stretch the children to think of many different active leisure time pursuits.

Hike Along
Hungarian Folk Song

Take a pack and we'll go hik-ing, Find a hid-den
There's a stream that's ev-er wind-ing to a gol-den

Fine

path-way in the woods we know. Sing-ing, sing-ing as we go a-long;
mea-dow as the soft winds blows.

D.C. al Fine

Foot-steps ech-o-ing our hik-ing song.

Verse 2:

Climb to where the clouds are passing
Close enough to touch a field of new-mown hay.
Singing, singing as we go along,
Footsteps echoing our hiking song.
Down below a bright spring ripples,
Soon the valley beckons and we're on our way.

Here is a new verse about autumn:

In the fall the leaves start turning;
Squirrels are storing nuts for winter's blanket white.
Birds fly south to find a warmer clime;
Nature shows her colors at this time.
In the woods the campfire's burning,
Lighting up our faces in the autumn night.

GA1522

To Fall or Not to Fall

Children are to look at these pictures and notice what's in each picture. You may wish to discuss each picture with the class as a whole. Then tell them to color only the pictures that have some connection with fall. Any other pictures are not to be colored. If some picture is colored that doesn't seem appropriate for fall, the teacher should ask the child for the connection. Teachers may learn of connections not obvious to the adult eye. (Correct answers: 1, 3, 4, 5, 8).
Copy this part of the page.

GA1522

Song of the Crow
Chinese Folk Song

Quickly

"Caw, caw, caw!" says the crow to me. He loves the "old ones," I can see.

Birds grow— old so they can`t fly, Son flut-ters out, some— worms to spy.

Mo-ther dear he— feeds with care; He ne-ver minds he has-n`t a share,

My mo-ther dear she once fed me. "Caw!" says the crow up— in the tree.

Here is a different verse to sing using the tune of "Song of the Crow":

Grandparents' Day
"I love you," Grandma says to me;
She gives her time so happily.
Grandpa is always lots of fun,
He listens 'til my story's done.
Grandparents seem to understand;
When I need help they lend a hand.
I love my grandma, grandpa too.
I want to help them in what they do.

Grandparents' Day is the second Sunday in September. As "Song of the Crow" illustrates, children should try to help their parents and grandparents. In China elders are highly respected for their knowledge and wisdom. Many grandparents live in the same home with their grandchildren in China.

Have each child interview a grandparent, an elderly relative, or an elderly friend of the family using the Interview Sheet on the next page. Allow plenty of time to complete this exercise since some may need to send a copy of the Interview Sheet by mail to a grandparent and wait for a response. Share the responses with the class by having the children read them aloud.

GA1522

They may discover commonalities between their lives and those of their grandparents, or that the differences make the grandparent more interesting and understandable.

Interview Sheet

1. What was your grade school like?

2. What games did you play at my age?

3. What sports did you play at my age (if any)?

4. What kind of music was popular when you were my age? What kind of music do you like to listen to now?

5. Did you have a bicycle?

6. What styles of clothing did you wear at my age?

7. What kinds of toys did you play with?

8. What was your favorite holiday back then? Now?

GA1522

October

GA1522

Ahrirang
Korean Folk Song

Ah - ri - rang, Ah - ri - rang, Ah - ra - ri - yo,_____ walk - ing o - ver

roll-ing hills___ of___ Ah - ri - rang.   Walk - ing   slow-ly   to   some place___ far,___

far a - way,   Hop - ing to re - turn a - gain to Ah - ri - rang___ some   day.

Verse 2:

> Ahrirang, Ahrirang, Ahrariyo,
> Time goes very slowly far away from Ahrirang.
> Back again over tall hills of Ahrirang,
> Once again returning home to Ahrirang.

These new words will help children learn the colors in the spectrum of the rainbow. It is sung to the tune of "Ahrirang."

Roy G. Biv

Roy G. Biv, Roy G. Biv, Roy G. Biv,
Colors of the rainbow spell Roy G. Biv.
R—red, O—orange, Y—yellow, G for green,
B is blue, I—indigo, V for violet's sheen.

Roy G. Biv, Roy G. Biv, Roy G. Biv,
People of the earth are like a rainbow too.
Many colors each day living side by side,
All together shining different lights to guide.

Make the children aware that each letter in the name of Roy G. Biv represents a color in the order it appears in the light spectrum of the rainbow. Put the name Roy G. Biv on the board and have the children tell what color each letter stands for. They will have sung it already in the song. Help them remember about indigo and violet by singing the song again if they have trouble with those two. Indigo is a dark to grayish-purple color. Rainbows are formed when beams of sunlight strike falling raindrops at just the right angle. The drops act like tiny prisms to separate the beams of light into individual bands of color. Ordinary light is actually a blend of all the colors of the rainbow!

GA1522

Copy the picture of Roy G. Biv and have the children color him using only the colors of the rainbow spectrum. Have older children draw their own character of Roy G. Biv and color him using only the seven colors of the rainbow spectrum.

34

Harvest
Danish Folk Song

When all the leaves are turn-ing brown and ap-ple trees are bend-ing down, it's time to pick the ap-ples sweet and ga-ther in the har-vest. Come and pick the ap-ples sweet, ap-ples sweet, ap-ples sweet. Reach up high and don't be shy or you will be the last to eat.

These new verses sung to the tune of "Harvest" will teach children about noun and verb agreement.

Noun and Verb Must Both Agree

Verse 1: When I use nouns and verbs to write
Like "We was out to fly a kite."
The noun and verb must both agree,
"We were" is what it should be!

Refrain: Noun and verb must both agree, both agree, both agree.
Get it right; don't let them fight, and
You can learn it easily!

Verse 2: When I use nouns and verbs to speak
Like "They was playing hide and seek."
The noun and verb must both agree,
"They were" is what it should be!

Refrain: Plural versus singular, singular, singular.
Get it right; don't let them fight!
Know when you should use *was* or *were*!

GA1522

Harvesting Verbs

Singular nouns require singular verbs. Plural nouns require plural verbs. Read the sentences below. Then pick the correct apple with the correct verb on it for each sentence. Cut it out and paste it in the blank space.

Copy this part for the students to cut and paste.

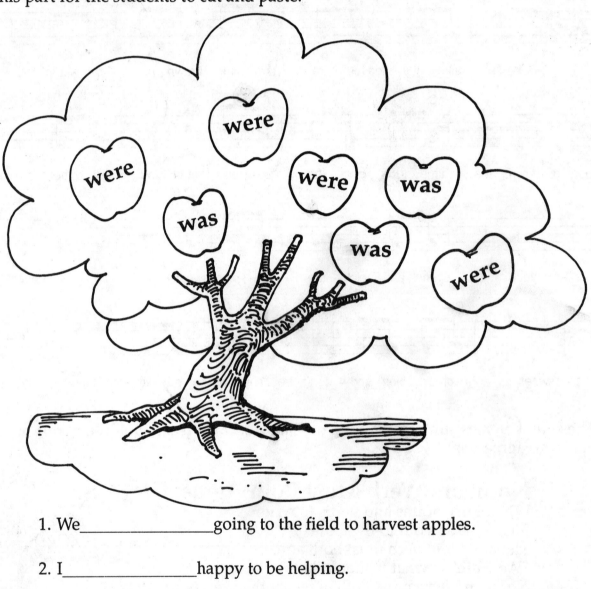

1. We_____going to the field to harvest apples.

2. I_____happy to be helping.

3. Both the ladder and bucket_____used to gather apples.

4. Neither Bobby nor Billy_____there to help that day.

5. Either my dad or brothers_____going to bring lunch.

6. Mom_____working in the kitchen to prepare our lunch.

7. The apples_____red, ripe, and sweet.

36

Bella Bimba
Folk Song from Italy

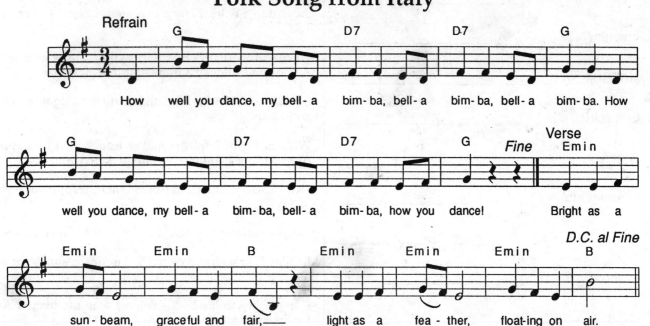

Verse 2:

Whirling and twirling,
Round and around,
Feet always moving
When music sounds.

Here is a new song that will tell children about Christopher Columbus since Columbus Day is really October 12. These words are to be sung to the tune of "Bella Bimba."

Columbus

Columbus sailed across the ocean, 'cross the ocean, 'cross the ocean,
Columbus sailed across the ocean, 'cross the ocean seeking land.
He had a theory the earth was round.
By sailing westward land could be found.
The fleet he had was only three ships, only three ships, only three ships.
The fleet he had was only three ships, only three ships from Spain.

Famous Places—Famous Faces!

Here is a fun activity for older students that will make them more aware of historical figures (like Columbus) and geography. They are to look at the list of famous places and then read about the famous faces (people). Some of the places were actually named for these famous people; others might remind them of famous people. They are to write the name of the famous person next to the place in the blank provided. Use of a dictionary, encyclopedia, map, or atlas is encouraged. Extend the exercise by having them make up their own matching game using towns or cities they find while using an atlas or map. Let them trade their newly created game with another student for his or her newly created game!

37

Famous Places

1. Washington, DC _____

2. Lincoln, NE _____

3. Houston, TX _____

4. Columbus, OH _____

5. America _____

6. Jackson, MS _____

7. Bismarck, ND _____

8. Monroe, LA _____

9. Jefferson City, MO _____

10. La Salle, CO _____

11. Madison, WI _____

12. Pontiac, MI _____

13. Raleigh, NC _____

14. St. Augustine, FL _____

15. Tecumseh, OK _____

16. Pennsylvania _____

17. Franklin, NH _____

18. Lafayette, OR _____

19. Hancock, NY _____

20. Carson City, NV _____

21. Carver, KY _____

22. Cortez, CO _____

Famous Faces

Prince Otto Eduard Leopold von Bismarck: First Chancellor of the German Empire

Sieur de La Salle: French explorer of North America in the 1600s

Hernando Cortez: Spanish explorer, conqueror of the Aztecs, and colonial administrator of New Spain

Sir Walter Raleigh: English courtier, navigator, colonizer, and writer

William Penn: English Quaker leader who was appointed proprietor of a commonwealth in America

"Kit" Carson: American frontiersman, trapper, Indian agent, and guide

James Madison: Fourth President of the United States

Benjamin Franklin: American statesman, author, and scientist

Christopher Columbus: Explorer who discovered America for the Europeans

Saint Augustine: An early Christian church father and author

George Washington: First President of the United States, "Father of Our Country"

Marquis de Lafayette: French military and political leader who commanded American troops in the Revolutionary War

Thomas Jefferson: Third President of the United States

Amerigo Vespucci: Italian navigator who explored the New World coastline after Columbus

George Washington Carver: African-American agricultural chemist and educator

John Hancock: First Governor of state of Massachusetts; American statesman and first signer of the Declaration of Independence

Sam Houston: American General and President of the Republic of Texas twice

Pontiac: Native American Indian Chief of the Ottawa tribe in the 1700s

Andrew Jackson: Seventh President of the United States

James Monroe: Fifth President of the United States

Abraham Lincoln: Sixteenth President of the United States

Tecumseh: Native American Indian leader and Chief of the Shawnee tribe who tried to unite Indians against whites

GA1522

A Fable
Winnebago Song

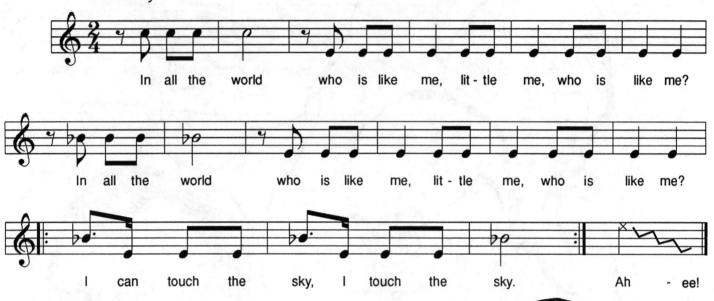

Boastfully

In all the world who is like me, lit-tle me, who is like me?

In all the world who is like me, lit-tle me, who is like me?

I can touch the sky, I touch the sky. Ah - ee!

Here is a new verse sung to the tune of "A Fable."

On Halloween

On Halloween I wear a mask on my face so I'm not me.
On Halloween I wear a mask on my face so I'm not me.
I can be just what I want to be!
I can be just what I want to be! Ah-eee!

Masks are used in nearly all cultures for a variety of purposes. They have been used in numerous religious practices. They have also been used in cultural ceremonies and rituals. In many instances, masks have been used for recreational and entertainment purposes. Masks allow the wearer to take on a new identity.

Friendship Masks

Create masks of teachers, principal, or staff in the school using paper plates or sacks. All students should wear the masks and let the other children in the class guess who they are. They may give clues by talking and acting like that person if the children have trouble identifying them.

Suggested materials to use to decorate the masks are yarn, crayons, cardboard tubing, eyeglasses, fake mustache, pieces of construction paper, etc. Exaggeration should be encouraged since these masks are like caricatures of real people. Remind the students that this is all to be done in good fun. Later the "Friendship Masks" are given to that person as a gift.

GA1522

Halloween Round
French Folk Tune

What's to do on Hall - o - ween? Fun and fro - lic and stunts a - plen - ty!

What's to do on Hall - o - ween? Ho, ho, for Hall - o - ween!

Verse 2:

Wear a costume and a mask. Fun and frolic and stunts a-plenty! Wear a costume and a mask. Ho, ho, for Halloween!

Verse 3:

Go a-calling "Trick or treat!" Fun and frolic and stunts a-plenty! Go a-calling "Trick or treat!" Ho, ho, for Halloween!

The Monster from the Haunted House

This haunted house is made up of many different shapes. There are triangles, squares, rectangles, circles, ovals, diamonds, crescents, etc. Look at your copy of the haunted house and try to see shapes that you can cut out and use to construct your very own monster. Cut the haunted house shapes apart and place them on a piece of construction paper. Arrange them and play with them in different patterns with the goal of constructing a Halloween monster from them. When you get them arranged exactly like you want, glue them on the construction paper. Then go back and color your monster pieces if you want. No two will look exactly the same. Display these monsters on a bulletin board.

The Haunted House

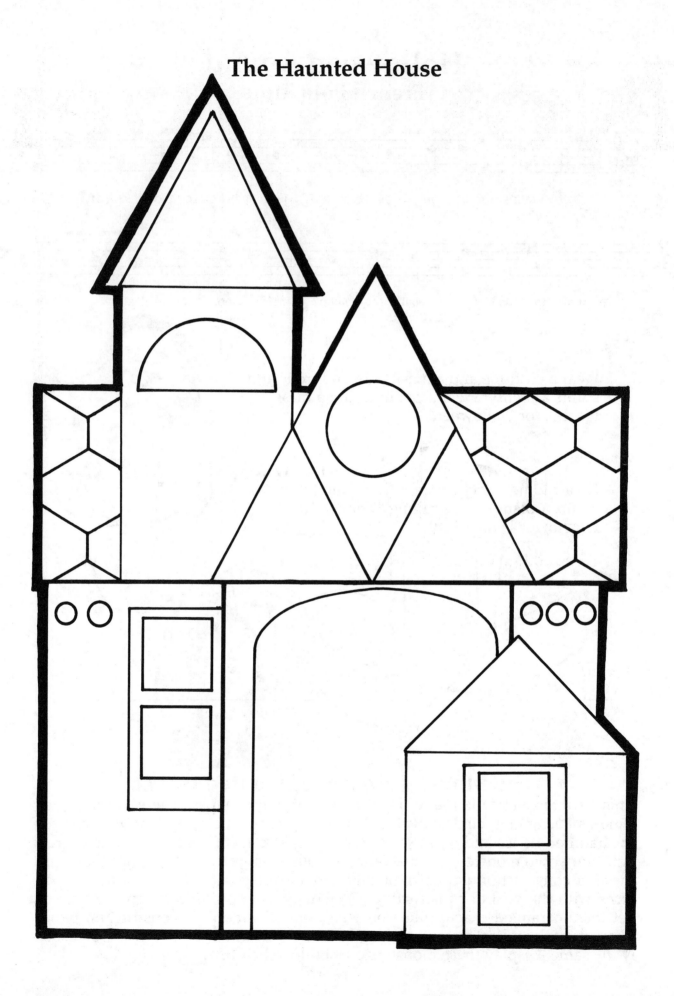

42

November

43

GA1522

Fiesta!
Mexican Folk Tune

Lively

O - le!   O - le!   Fi - es-ta be-gins to - day;   O -

le!   O - le!   We'll dance and we'll sing and play;   O - le!   O -

le!   Our trou-bles we'll throw a - way;   O - le!   O - le!   We'll

dance to the mu - sic gay.   Oh, what fun to go danc-ing to - ge - ther, with a

swing and a sway and a twirl!   Ev - 'ry step is as light as a

fea - ther,   oh, what fun to go 'round in a whirl!

Verse 2:

Ole! Ole! Guitar and a violin,
Ole! Ole! Maracas and mandolin;
Ole! Ole! The marketplace rings with sound,
Ole! Ole! Come dance all around and 'round.

Repeat refrain.

44

GA1522

Here is a new verse sung to the tune of "Fiesta."
This verse will get the children interested in
Election Day activities.

Election Day!
Go vote! Go vote! For this is Election Day,
Go vote! Go vote! Go early and don't delay!
Go vote! Go vote! It's time to say yea or nay;
Go vote! Go vote! Be sure that you have your say!
Oh, which candidates will you be choosing?
Did the issues they spoke of concern you?
It's a day full of winning and losing;
Voting is something we all should do!

Election Elation
In the United States, elections of some kind are held every year. Some elections are to place people into public offices, and some are to decide questions of what the majority prefers. A day set aside for elections as stated in the Constitution of the United States is the first Tuesday after the first Monday in November.

The election of the President of the United States happens every four years, while the election of a United States Senator happens only every six years. Every citizen should consider very carefully how to vote.

United States citizens must be registered before they are allowed to vote. That means people must have their names placed in a special Voter Registration Book before the day of the election.

On Election Day, people who have not taken the time to register to vote may not vote since their names do not appear in the official book.

On Election Day registered voters travel to places to vote called polls where they receive a ballot which is a list of people or issues to be voted on. If voters are registered, they may vote by marking their choices on their ballots.

Once the polls close and the ballots are counted, election results are made known to the public as soon as possible.

Hold a mock election in your own classroom on Election Day. A week before Election Day have all students who want to vote register their names and have a teacher or a selected student print all of the names in a special Voter Registration Book. Remind the students that if their name does not appear in this book on Election Day, they will not be allowed to vote.

GA1522

During the week before the election, put up a sample ballot so students may see what is to be voted on. Students may campaign to promote their favored choices in the categories listed on the ballot. Campaign posters, buttons, and speeches should be encouraged during that week.

When Election Day arrives, the teacher should have students sign their names next to their names in the Voter Registration Book. At that time they're given a ballot. Have each student mark the ballot and put it in a ballot box. Assign three students to count and tally the ballot results. Announce the results once all ballots have been counted.

Feel free to let the students create their own ballots with other categories.

Copy this ballot for each registered voter.

Ballot

Holiday:
- ❏ Christmas
- ❏ Easter
- ❏ Fourth of July
- ❏ Halloween

Sport:
- ❏ Baseball
- ❏ Basketball
- ❏ Football
- ❏ Soccer

Season:
- ❏ Fall
- ❏ Spring
- ❏ Summer
- ❏ Winter

Style of Music:
- ❏ Classical
- ❏ Country
- ❏ Rap
- ❏ Rock 'n' Roll

GA1522

Matilda
Jamaican Folk Tune

Matilda, Matilda, Matilda, she take me money and run Venezuela.

Five thousand dollars, friend, I lost. The woman even take me cart and horse. Matilda, she take me money and run Venezuela.

Verse 2: My money was to buy me house and land,
The woman she got a serious plan.
Matilda, she take me money and run Venezuela.
Refrain

Verse 3: Now the money was safe in me bed,
Stuck in the pillow beneath me head,
But Matilda, she find me money and run Venezuela.
Refrain

Verse 4: Never will I love again,
All me money gone in vain
'Cause Matilda, she take me money and run Venezuela.
Refrain

Here is a new song about compound words sung to the tune of "Matilda":

Compound Words

Refrain: Compound words, compound words,
Compound words, two words together can form a compound word!

Verse 1: Thanksgiving is a compound word.
The bluebird and goldfinch are some I've heard.
Compound words, two words together can form a compound word.

GA1522

Refrain
Verse 2:   Somebody is a compound word.
                   A boyfriend and a girlfriend are some I've heard.
                   Compound words, two words together can form a
                   compound word.
Refrain

Compound Chain Gangs

Divide the class into four groups or "chain gangs." Explain that each chain gang is to gather points for their group by writing as many compound words stemming from the previous compound word in the chain. This compound word chain is built and scored according to which part of the previous compound word is used to come up with the next compound word. Using the first half of the compound word achieves one point. Using the second half achieves five points. Each group will be given the same compound word to begin the chain. Write it on the chalkboard, on the overhead projector, or on a sheet of paper for each group to see. You may wish to demonstrate how a compound word chain is made and scored before starting the game. For instance, if each group began with the word *horseback*, one chain gang could perhaps come up with this chain of compound words:

backhoe   hoedown   downhill   hillside   sidestep   stepson   stepchild
(5 points) (5 points) (5 points) (5 points) (5 points) (5 points) (1 point)

Points for that chain are 31. The chain could just as easily have taken a different direction. Set a time limit of 5 minutes for each group to work on their chain. Only one person should write the words in the chain for the group. Use of a dictionary by each chain gang is encouraged. The group with the highest points at the end of the game is declared the winner, but everyone wins because everyone is learning.

Image-Creative Compound Words

Form a brand-new word by putting two words together. Draw your own picture of what you imagine your new creative compound word to look like. Even real compound words may be used with creative illustrations. See the examples on the next page. Then draw your own in the blank squares provided.

GA1522

Eyeglass	Dogflower

GA1522

Hush, Little Baby
African-American Folk Tune

Hush, lit-tle ba-by, don`t say a word,

Ma-ma`s goin` to buy you a mock-ing-bird.

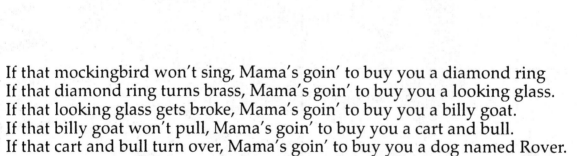

If that mockingbird won't sing, Mama's goin' to buy you a diamond ring
If that diamond ring turns brass, Mama's goin' to buy you a looking glass.
If that looking glass gets broke, Mama's goin' to buy you a billy goat.
If that billy goat won't pull, Mama's goin' to buy you a cart and bull.
If that cart and bull turn over, Mama's goin' to buy you a dog named Rover.
If that dog named Rover won't bark, Mama's goin' to buy you a horse and cart.
If that horse and cart fall down, you'll still be the prettiest one in town.

Here are new words sung to the tune of "Hush, Little Baby":

Thanksgiving Day
Thanksgiving Day is a time to say, "Thanks," for the things that have come our way.
'Round the table we all sit down, our house fills with happy sound.
Our relatives come from far and near, some we haven't seen in about a year.
Playing with cousins is lots of fun; through the chilly air we like to run.
Smells from the kitchen tease my nose, thinking of the food as my hunger grows.
I have so much to be thankful for; how could anyone ask for more?

What I'm Thankful for in Alphabetical Order

Have the children tell or write down a list of things they're thankful for, using each letter of the alphabet in alphabetical order. Each blessing they're thankful for needs to begin with the letter of the alphabet found on the different items spilling out of the cornucopia below. This activity can be done as a group with the teacher calling on individual students and writing their responses. Or students can write their own lists individually. If done individually, give them a chance to share and compare their lists with the other class members' lists. Copy the cornucopia for each student.

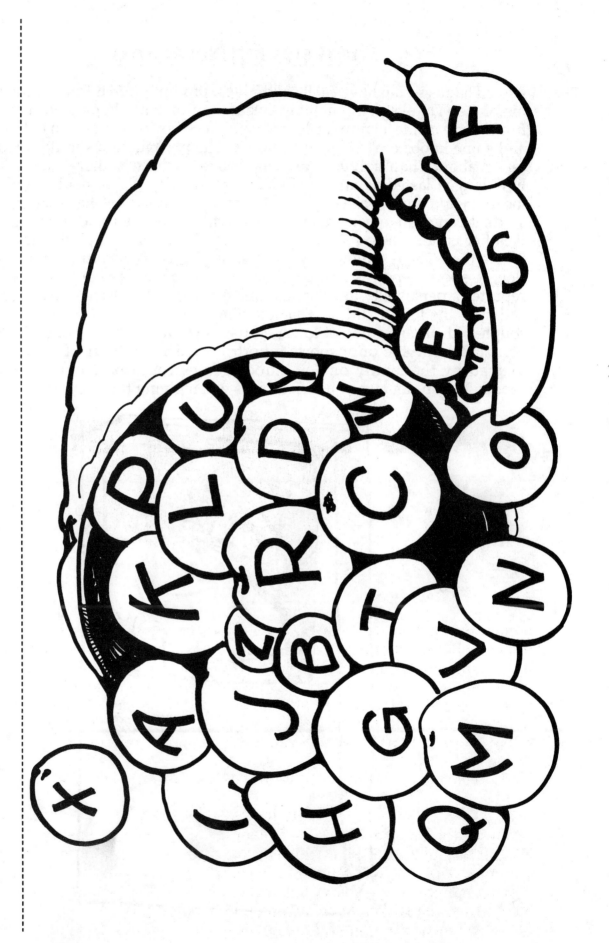

51

Thanksgiving News Reviews

After Thanksgiving have each child give a presentation in front of the class about his or her Thanksgiving holiday celebration or what happened. It can be quite fun if done inside a large cardboard appliance box with a screen cut out like a TV and some knobs drawn on and colored. The presentation should include a news report about Thanksgiving Day: who cooked, who was there, where it was held, how long it lasted, what foods were served, why it was held in that particular location, and any special customs the family observes at Thanksgiving. The same student can change personality into a weather reporter and give a report on the weather conditions on Thanksgiving Day. He or she may wish to use maps of where their Thanksgiving Day took place. Humor is encouraged in the presentation. A sports report is also possible. The same student could then don a sports reporter's personality and/or costume or disguise and tell of any sports-related activities the family did on Thanksgiving, such as, "The Carter family played a rough-and-tumble game of touch football in Grandfather Carter's backyard." Of course, maybe the only sports report needed is a report of what sports were viewed by the family on TV. Indoor games could be included in the sports report. The students may use notecards when giving their reports.

GA1522

Boker
Israeli Children's Song

Morn- ing, morn- ing, bright and cheer- ful morn- ing;
Morn- ing, morn- ing, good morn - ing ev - 'ry - one! The
dawn has come, and work's be- gun. We plow and sow be- neath the sun. Our
work is hard, but we are strong. When morn - ing comes a - long.

2. Noontime, noontime, a happy afternoon time!
   Noontime, noontime, good cheer to ev'ryone!
   We'll wash and pray, oh what a treat to thank our God before we eat!
   Praised be Thou with song and mirth for food from this, our earth!

3. Evening, evening, 'tis dark, the sun is leaving!
   Evening, evening, shalom to ev'ryone.
   The day is done, and rest is nigh. The moon and stars are in the sky,
   We'll sing and dance and each feel gay, for evening's on the way!

4. Nighttime, nighttime, to bed, to bed, the right time!
   Nighttime, nighttime, good night to ev'ryone!
   We pray to Thee, O Lord above, for Mom and Dad and all Thy love.
   Bless us, too, with all Thy might. Good night, good night, sleep tight!

Here are two new verses sung to the tune of "Boker":

1. Turkey, dressing, hot and tasty dressing, gravy, green beans,
   there's some for ev'ryone!
   The food is done, the feast's begun, the cooks deserve an ovation!
   I've piled my plate so very high; I hope there's room for pie!

2. Next-door neighbors, our friendly next-door neighbors
   don't eat turkey; they're vegetarians!
   Tofu they eat instead of meat; for healthy food it's hard to beat.
   With vegetables they fill their plates, but they still celebrate!

GA1522

Vegetarianism

Vegetarians are people who practice a diet that excludes meat and meat products. Many vegetarians do eat breads, cereals, rice, pasta, fruits, vegetables, milk, yogurt, cheese, beans, eggs, nuts, and sweets. Vegans are people who have a diet similar to vegetarians except that they do not eat any animal products. For instance, they do not eat cheese (unless it contains no animal products), milk, ice cream, eggs, yogurt, or even honey.

Look at the foods below and color all of the foods that a vegetarian would eat. Then cut out the foods that a vegan would eat and paste them on a piece of construction paper. They will already be colored.

Tasting for Themselves

Let the children experience eating a food that vegans and vegetarians eat: tofu hot dogs. Tofu is made out of soybeans and provides lots of protein. Bring some tofu hot dogs to school and let children taste them. Cut them into small chunks and serve using toothpicks as utensils. Let the children dip them in mustard or catsup. Have the children look at them and tell what they see (hot dogs). After they've tasted them, discuss how they tasted. Then reveal what they're made of. If tofu hot dogs or meatless hot dogs are not available at the local grocery store, they can usually be purchased at health food stores in the frozen foods section.

Copy the part below for the students. Have them circle the answers they believe are correct. Then read the correct answers to them. They may be very surprised by the answers! (Answer key for the teacher's eyes only: 1. 20, 2. 80, 3. 55 sq. ft., 4. 25, 5. 2500, 6. 6, 7. 55, 8. 20,000, 9. 165, 10. 16)

Copy this part of the page

----

1. Percentage of corn grown in the United States eaten by people:

   30   20   40

2. Percentage of corn grown in the United States eaten by livestock:

   80   70   60

3. Area of tropical rain forest consumed in every quarter-pound hamburger:

   25 sq. ft.   40 sq. ft.   55 sq. ft.

4. Gallons of water used to produce a pound of wheat:

   5   15   25

5. Gallons of water used to produce a pound of meat:

   1000   2000   2500

6. Percentage of pesticide residues in the United States diet supplied by vegetables:

   10   6   3

7. Percentage of pesticide residues in the United States diet supplied by meat:

   25   45   55

8. Pounds of potatoes that can be grown on an acre of land:

   200   2000   20,000

9. Pounds of beef produced on an acre of land:

   165   3000   10,000

10. Pounds of grain and soybeans needed to produce a pound of feedlot beef:

    7   10   16

GA1522

Famous Vegetarians

Fill in the vowels to find out who these famous vegetarians are. Some are historical figures while others are still very much alive. See how many of them you've
heard of and discuss as a group what they did or do now. (Answer key for the
teacher's eyes only: 1. Mister Rogers, children's TV show host; 2. Paul McCart-
ney, rock musician; 3. Tony LaRussa, manager of the Oakland Athletics baseball
team; 4. Madonna, pop singer; 5. Albert Einstein, physicist; 6. Michael Jackson,
pop singer/dancer; 7. Daryl Hannah, movie star; 8. Socrates, philosopher; 9. Leo
Tolstoy, writer; 10. Henry David Thoreau, writer; 11. Mahatma Gandhi, politi-
cian/statesman; 12. Doug Henning, magician; 13. Johnny Cash, country singer;
14. Chubby Checker, rock 'n' roll singer; 15. Peter Gabriel, rock musician;
16. Thomas Alva Edison, inventor; 17. David Bowie, rock singer; 18. k.d. lang,
pop/country singer; 19. Hayley Mills, actress; 20. Dave Scott, six-time winner of
the Ironman Triathlon; 21. Percy Shelley, poet; 22. Leonardo da Vinci,
painter/inventor; 23. Pythagoras, mathematics philosopher; 24. Casey Kasem,
radio disc jockey; 25. Chris Campbell, 1992 Olympic Bronze Medal winner in
wrestling)

Copy this part for the students:

----

1. M__ st__ r R__ g__ rs

2. P__ __l McC__ rtn__ y

3. T__ ny L__ R__ ss__

4. M__ d__ nn__

5. __ lb__ rt __ __ nst__ __n

6. M__ ch__ __l J__ cks__ n

7. D__ ryl H__ nn__ h

8. S__ cr__ t__ s

9. L__ __ T__ lst__ y

10. H__ nry D__ v__ d Th__ r__ __ __

11. M__ h__ tm__ G__ ndh__

12. D__ __ g H__ nn__ ng

13. J__ hnny C__ sh

14. Ch__ bby Ch__ ck__ r

15. P__ t__ r G__ br__ __l

16. Th__ m__ s __lv__ __ d__ s__ n

17. D__ v__ d B__ w__ __

18. k.d. l__ ng

19. H__ yl__ y M__ lls

20. D__ v__ Sc__ tt

21. P__ rcy Sh__ ll__ y

22. L__ __ n__ rd__ d__ V__ nci

23. Pyth__ g__ r__ s

24. C__ s__ y K__ s__ m

25. Chr__ s C__ mpb__ ll

GA1522

Lonely Is the Hogan
Navajo Indian Song

Lone - ly is the ho - gan,____ The birds are still.

No more____ the wild flow - ers bloom on the hill.

Verse 2:

>   White upon the mesa the winter snow,
>   Cold blows the wind through the canyon below.

Here are two new verses sung to the tune of "Lonely Is the Hogan":

Beauty Is Created

1. Beauty is created; just visualize;
   Picture a creation before your eyes.

2. Whether you are weaving or using clay,
   Just let your hands and your mind show the way.

Talent and Art Show

Beauty can be created in many ways. Letting the children have their own Talent and Art Show will illustrate this to them. Some may want to show paintings or drawings which could be on display for the rest of the class to see. Other students will want to take a more dynamic approach such as reading a poem, dancing, playing an instrument, singing, doing a magic show, or presenting a comedy act or short skit. It's best to leave this activity open-ended to allow the students as much creativity as possible. They should be allowed to work in small groups for their talent presentation if they so desire. They will enjoy being able to define what they consider art and/or talent. Put up a poster about the Talent and Art Show that advertises the event to spark their interest. Then let them sign up for whatever talent or art project they want to do. Don't force anyone to perform who really doesn't want to; this should be a fun activity for the audience as well as for the performers.

GA1522

December

58

Joyous Chanukah
Hebrew Folk Song

Cha-nu-kah, Cha-nu-kah, hol-i-day so fair, Glow-ing light, can-dles bright,

hap-pi-ness we share. Gai-ly dance, gai-ly sing while the drei-del whirls,

Round and round, round and round, see how fast it twirls.

Here is an alternative verse sung to the tune of "Joyous Chanukah":

Spin the Top!

Spin the top, spin the top, A E I O U.
When it falls it shows vowels; use one as your cue.
Make a word with that vowel; many points you'll earn.
Ev'ry word has a vowel; it's fun while you learn!

GA1522

Enlarge and copy the dreidel, have the children each cut out one dreidel, fold down the points, and tape together. Ideally, each child will be able to construct a vowel dreidel to use with the dreidel games listed. Here are several ideas to use with these vowel dreidels.

Vowels Around the World

Each child spins a dreidel one at a time and whatever vowel it lands on represents a city, state, or country that must be named. For instance, *A* could be Antarctica; *E* could be England; *I* could be India; *O* could be Ottawa; and *U* could be Uganda. Each time the vowel appears in the name, a point is scored. Therefore, Antarctica earns 3 points since it has 3 *A*'s in it. At the end of the first round, those tied with the highest points go another round. Each new round involves spinning the dreidel. Rounds continue as long as there are tie scores. The game and rounds end when one person is the highest point scorer. Several games may be played at just one sitting.

A variation of the dreidel game could be for children to select a category before each spin. After a dreidel lands on a vowel, points are earned by naming a word containing that vowel in the selected category. Categories should be listed on the board before the game begins. Here are a few examples to get the list started: sports, animals, foods, holidays, people, clothing, television shows, furniture. Children should be encouraged to make up new categories to list on the board. If a child picks the category "animals," spins the dreidel, and it lands on an *O*, that child will need to think of an animal containing the letter *O*. *Monkey* contains the letter *O* and earns the child one point. *Octopus* contains the letter *O* twice, so it earns the child 2 points. Rounds continue with those tied to spin and play until a winner emerges.

Long and Short of It

Again, children spin their dreidels and whatever vowel is landed upon will have to be used in two words. One word will be using a short vowel and the other a long vowel. They earn a point for each designated vowel, but a bonus of 5 points if they can use both the long vowel and the short vowel in one word! For instance, *E* is rolled and the word *beaten* is used. The child gets one point for the long *E*, one point for the short *E*, and five points for using both in the same word. The total for that round is 7! Rounds work the same as in the previous dreidel games.

The Piñata
Mexican Folk Song

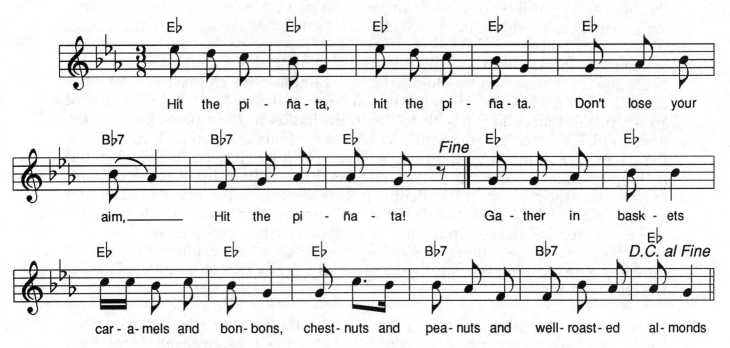

Hit the pi - ña - ta, hit the pi - ña - ta. Don't lose your aim, _____ Hit the pi - ña - ta! *Fine* Ga - ther in bask - ets car - a - mels and bon - bons, chest - nuts and pea - nuts and well - roast - ed al - monds *D.C. al Fine*

Verse 2:

Hit the piñata, hit the piñata.
Don't lose your aim, hit the piñata!
Sugared pineapples, apples to eat, now,
All of the guests will partake of the treat, now.
Hit the piñata, hit the piñata,
Don't lose your aim, hit the piñata!

Here is a new song sung to the tune of "The Piñata":

Small Words in Large Words

Small words in large words, small words in large words,
Look and you'll find them, small words in large words.

Look at *together*; you'll find it has three:
To, get, and her; it's easy, you see.

Small words in large words, small words in large words,
Look and you'll find them, small words in large words.

Look at the prefix; it's at the beginning;
Notice the suffix; it's there at the ending.

Small words in large words, small words in large words,
Look and you'll find them, small words in large words.

GA1522

Prefix/Suffix Piñata

Load a good-sized basket with slips of paper which have words written on them that will accept at least one prefix or suffix to make a new word. Have enough slips so that each child in the class will get one once they are dumped out.

Suspend the basket with a string tied to it so that it hangs above the children's heads like a piñata. Choose a child to be "it." Blindfold the child, spin him or her around, and give him or her a yardstick to strike at the basket. Set a time limit of 10 seconds. If that child is unable to dump the basket in 10 seconds, go on to the next child. Continue playing until the basket contents are dumped. As soon as the papers are dumped on the floor, everyone will be allowed to scramble and pick up one slip of paper. After everyone sits down with a slip of paper containing a word, students will work silently at their desks to list as many prefixes and suffixes that can be added to their word in 5 minutes. Each word made will earn one point. Remind the children that a prefix is a syllable, group of syllables, or a word joined to the beginning of another word to alter its meaning or to create a new meaning. A suffix is basically the same as a prefix except that it is placed at the end of a word.

Here is a list of possible words to be used for the basket/piñata game: *place, small, joy, appoint, active, pay, great, play, friend, complete, hope, common, charge, regular, long, mix, slow, member, port, plant, truth, help, tent, press, mission, kind.*

Some common prefixes: *ex, ad, com, con, de, dis, anti, hyper, in, inter, mis, di, ab, ante, un*

Some common suffixes: *est, ment, er, ness, ly, ally, able, ible*

Mary Had a Baby
African-American Spiritual

Ma-ry had a ba-by, Yes, Lord, Ma-ry had a ba-by, Yes, my Lord,

Ma-ry had a ba-by, Yes, Lord, The peo-ple keep a-com-in' and the train done gone.

2. What did Mary name him? Yes, Lord.
What did Mary name him? Yes, my Lord.
What did Mary name him? Yes, Lord.
The people keep a-coming and the train has gone.

3. Mary named him Jesus . . .

4. Where was Jesus born . . .

5. Born in lowly stable . . .

6. Where did Mary lay him . . .

7. Laid him in a manger . . .

Here are several new verses sung to the tune of "Mary Had a Baby":

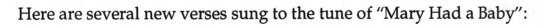

Christmas! Time for Safety!

1. Christmas! Time for safety. Yes, Lord!
Christmas! Time for safety. Yes, my Lord!
Christmas! Time for safety. Yes, Lord!
The holiday is better when you play it safe!

2. Just look at the light bulbs; don't touch!
Just look at the light bulbs; but don't touch!
Just look at the light bulbs; don't touch!
The holiday is better when you play it safe!

3. Watch out for the light cord; don't trip!
Watch out for the light cord; but don't trip!
Watch out for the light cord; don't trip!
The holiday is better when you play it safe!

4. Walk around the tree; don't run!
Walk around the tree; just don't run!
Walk around the tree; don't run!
The holiday is better when you play it safe!

5. Walk slowly on ice; don't fall!
Walk slowly on ice; just don't fall!
Walk slowly on ice; don't fall!
The holiday is better when you play it safe!

6. Careful with the ornaments; they'll break!
Careful with the ornaments; they may break!
Careful with the ornaments; they'll break!
The holiday is better when you play it safe!

GA1522

7. Stay away from candles; they burn!
   Stay away from candles; they will burn!
   Stay away from candles; they burn!
   The holiday is better when you play it safe!

Christmas Cautions!

Have the children listen to this story as you read it aloud and raise their hands each time they hear a holiday safety rule being violated. When they raise their hands, you should pause and have them identify the rule and why the rule is important to follow. They should also tell what "Pat" or "Joey" should have done instead.

Christmas morning was only a week away which made Pat very excited. He knew that today was the day his parents had planned to get a Christmas tree, and they would all get to decorate it when his dad got home from work. That afternoon when Pat, his mother, and little brother went to buy the Christmas tree, the sidewalks were slick with frozen ice from the storm the night before. Pat saw a very tall tree across the parking lot and ran towards it as fast as he could. Halfway to the tree, his feet shot out from under him on the ice and he fell hard. Pat's elbow began to hurt where he'd landed on it on the ice.

That evening when Dad came home, the whole family began decorating the tree. Pat asked his little brother, Joey, to give him one of the big, blue, round glass ornaments to hang on the tree. Joey removed it from the box and tossed it carelessly in Pat's direction. Pat wasn't ready to catch it and the ornament shattered on the hardwood floor. After Mom cleaned up the pieces of glass, Dad strung the lights all over the tree and plugged them in. The tree looked dazzling as the lights began to twinkle. However, Pat noticed that one of the light bulbs was not burning, so he grabbed the cord by the socket and tried to remove the bulb with his other hand. He suddenly felt a tingling jolt of electricity and he quickly let go of the cord and bulb.

Pat decided to sit on the couch beside the large Christmas candle his mother had lit earlier. He watched as presents were brought out of a back bedroom and placed under the tree. Joey couldn't decide where to put one of the gifts, and he began running in circles around the tree. His foot finally got caught in the electrical cord connected to the lights which nearly toppled the entire tree! Pat noticed a pool of liquid wax collecting at the base of the candle's flame. He tried sticking his finger in it to make the wax stick to it, but it was much hotter than he thought. He later had a blister on that same finger.

Pat, Joey, and their parents still had a good Christmas even with all the mishaps. And they learned that Christmas is a time to give, but not to give injuries to yourself or others!

O Christmas Tree
German Folk Song

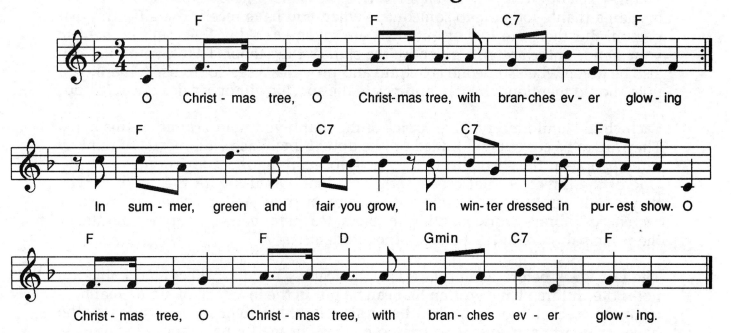

O Christ - mas tree, O Christ-mas tree, with bran-ches ev - er glow - ing

In sum - mer, green and fair you grow, In win - ter dressed in pur - est show. O

Christ - mas tree, O Christ - mas tree, with bran - ches ev - er glow - ing.

These new verses are sung to the tune of "O Christmas Tree":

Write Thank-You Notes

1. Write thank-you notes, write thank-you notes
For presents you've been given.
Write thank-you notes, write thank-you notes
For presents you've been given.

   The notes don't have to say a lot
   To show you're grateful for what you got.

   Write thank-you notes, write thank-you notes
   For presents you've been given.

2. Write thank-you notes, write thank-you notes
For presents you've been given.
Write thank-you notes, write thank-you notes
For presents you've been given.

   No matter if it's big or small
   You should acknowledge one and all.

   Write thank-you notes, write thank-you notes
   For presents you've been given.

GA1522

Thank-You Notes

Thank-you notes can be written for various reasons. One obvious reason to give or mail a thank-you note to someone is when you have received a gift from that person. But there are lots of gifts that are given each day that can't be held in your hand. These are gifts given by the staff of the school. Thank-you notes can also be given when someone is helpful and provides a service to us. A thank-you note should mention why you appreciate the specific gift or service given to you.

Each child should receive five copies of the thank-you note printed in this book. They are to be cut out and folded on the dotted line. Each child needs to think of three people at the school to write a note to thanking them for services or gifts. One of the three could also be another student. Discuss with the children who they might want to send thank-you notes to, such as janitors, cafeteria workers, secretaries, library workers, other teachers, teachers' helpers, parent volunteers, the principal, student teachers, or other students.

The last week before winter vacation, the teacher should collect any thank-you notes the children have written that can be put in the teachers' or staff's mailboxes in the teachers' lounge. Then he or she should deliver those. Students who have written to someone who has no mailbox in the lounge should be allowed time to deliver the note directly to that person. Make sure the students are reminded to take their extra blank thank-you notes home with them for the holidays to use for gifts they receive. They should be encouraged to copy more of these thank-you notes if they need them.

GA1522

GA1522

January

Troika Riding
Ukrainian Folk Song

Rapidly

O'er the ground we go a-fly-ing, Far be-yond the ci-ty ply-ing;

How I love to go a-rid-ing, Rid-ing in a troi-ka!

Hor-ses three, with hooves a-pound-ing, pull us on; a curve we're round-ing!

Win-ter's lots of fun for me when rid-ing in a troi-ka!

Verse 2:

'Round us swirls the snow a-flying,
Ice beneath the snow is lying;
Bundled up, don't mind the weather,
Snuggled in a troika!
Ev'ryone is out a-sleighing,
Skating, sliding, or just playing.
Winter's lots of fun for me when
Riding in a troika!

Here is a new song sung to the tune of "Troika Riding":

Winter Is a Fun Time

1. Start a ball of snow a-rolling,
   Push it, pack it, keep it growing.
   Use it for the snowman's bottom
   When we build a snowman.
   Next make one to be the middle,
   Then on top the head is little.
   Oh, what fun we have designing
   When we build a snowman!

GA1522

2. Think of games when it is snowing,
Call your friends so they'll be going.
Grab your sled and find a big hill.
Winter is a fun time!
Choose up sides and make some snow forts.
Don't get mad, but act like good sports.
We're so glad the snow has fallen;
Winter is a fun time!

Occupational Snowmen and Women

Give each child the snowman pattern from this book. Discuss what an occupation is (a job). Then tell children to decide what job this snowman or woman will do for a living, and then to draw the kind of clothing or accessories the snowman or woman would require for his or her career. Display occupational snowmen or women somewhere in the room. Label what career or occupation is represented.

Occupational Snowman or Woman Pattern

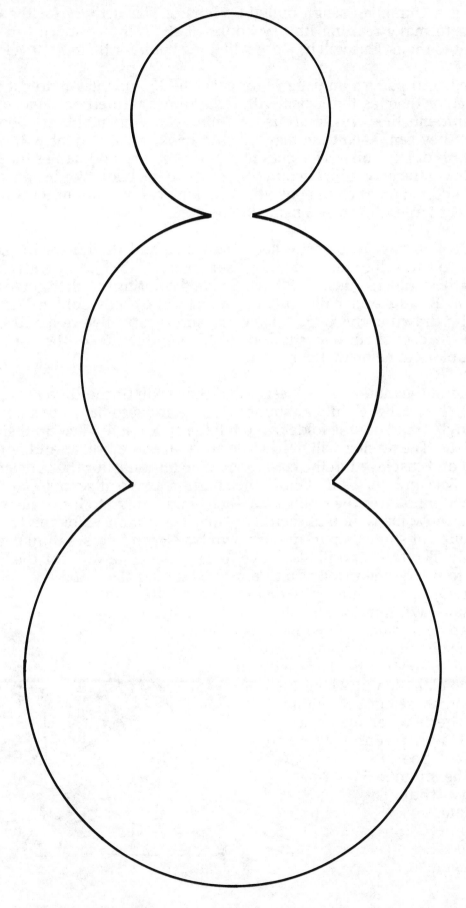

Literary Troika Race

A troika is a Ukrainian sleigh pulled by horses. This activity for the children is designed to make reading library books of their choice more fun and more important to them. This will be a good lifelong habit for them to develop.

Copy the troika pattern on page 73 for each child. Students are to cut the troikas out and color them as they wish with their names written on them somewhere. Tell the students they will have one month to read as many library books of their choice as they can. Each time they finish a book, each student will receive one horse for his or her troika. The student cuts out, colors, and names the horse after a character in the book or related in some way to the book. For instance, a horse's name related to a nonfiction book about making candles might be "Candlewax." The student writes the horse's name on the horse.

Each child will have a folder to keep the troika and the horses in. The teacher will need to keep all of the folders in a safe place. The children must be allowed access to their folders when they have finished coloring another horse after reading a book. Be sure each child puts his or her name on the folder. The horse pattern is also drawn in this book for the teacher to copy. Before handing a child a horse, the teacher should question the child as to the title of the book and what he or she plans to name that horse.

At the end of the month or the designated time span (it could go longer than just a month), the teacher should announce, "We're going to have our Literary Troika Race today!" Hand out the folders and tell the children to hitch up their horses to their troikas. The teacher will need to decide where the troikas and horses can be mounted and displayed in the classroom. One option is for the teacher to put all of the troikas and horses up before the children arrive at school that day. When the teacher announces the troika race, each child will go to his or her own troika and count how many horses there are. Another option is for the teacher to let small groups of students put up their own troikas and horses until everyone's is on display. The teacher will also have to provide some way for the children to mount their troikas and horses: staples, paste, tape, putty, etc. Once everything is on display, the children will count their own horses. The child with the most horses can be declared the winner. As a prize, the winner is allowed the opportunity if he or she so desires to share with the class an explanation of where each of his or her horses got its name. Of course, the teacher may want to think of a different prize and should feel free to reward the student any way that is appropriate.

Troika

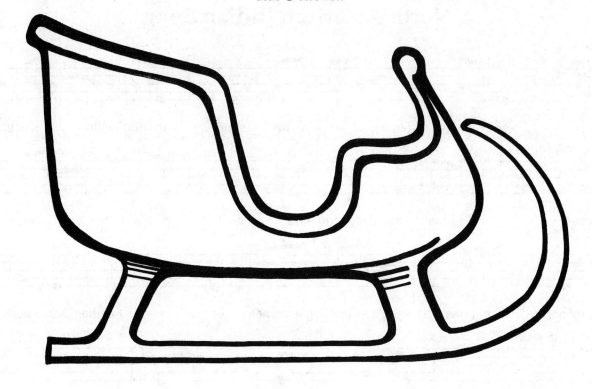

Horse

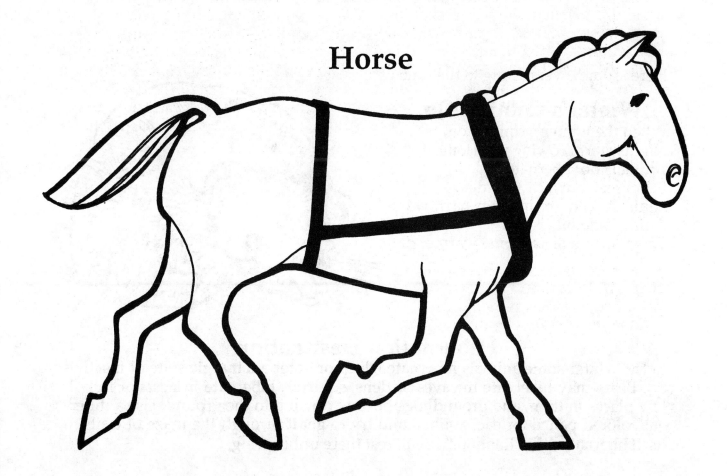

GA1522

Sunset
North American Indian Song

Now the moon___ is in the sky, to the sun___ we say good-
bye; Fa-ther Sun sleeps in the west. In the sky___ we see the
moon; sha-dows creep,___ the night comes soon. Fa-ther Sun sleeps in the
west, and his peo-ple go to___ rest.

Here is a new verse sung to the tune of "Sunset."

Winter's Coming On

When the winter's coming on,
Nights start growing very long.
Animals do hibernate.
Bears seek out a cave or den;
Squirrels and groundhogs burrow in.
Animals do hibernate.
They'll come out at some warmer date.

Hibernation Destination

In the winter some animals hibernate (sleep or enter a lethargic state of inactivity). Bears may hibernate in caves or dens, squirrels hibernate in nests or in hollow places in trees, and groundhogs burrow down into the ground. Use a different colored pencil for each animal and try to get it through the maze of trails to its "Hibernation Destination." It will rest there until spring.

GA1522

Hibernation Destination

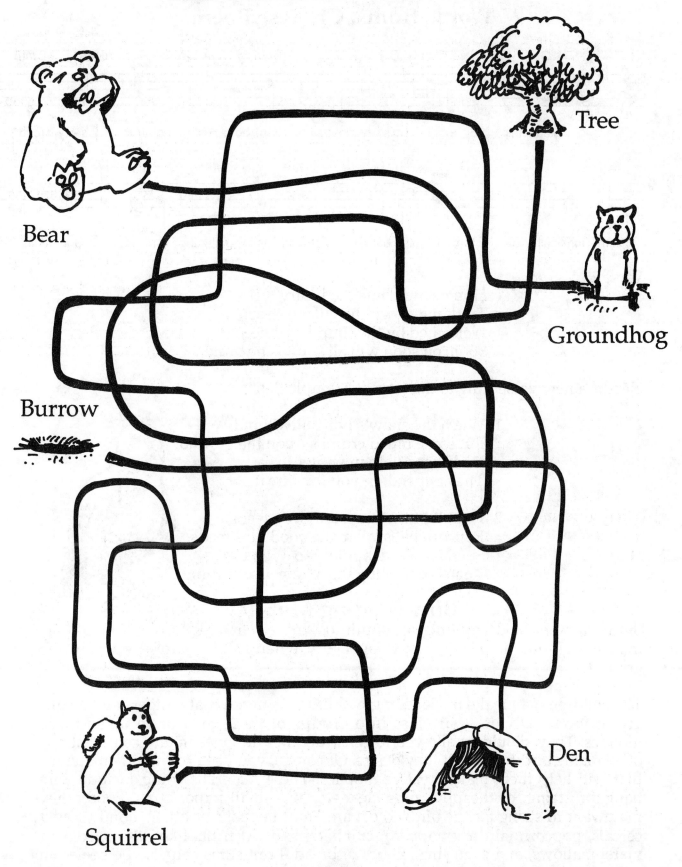

Bear

Tree

Groundhog

Burrow

Den

Squirrel

75

Temple Bell
Melody from China
Words from a Chinese Poem

Moun-tains hid in a mis-ty cloud; Bam-boos lin-ing the dus-ty road.

Chim-ing call of tem-ple bell; Night is fall-ing on field and dell.

Verse 2:

Homeward come the weary feet
Trudging down the village street,
Welcomed by the sound of flute.
Soon, oh soon will all sounds be mute.

Here is a new verse sung to the tune of "Temple Bell":

1. When the snow's lying all around,
   Put some bread crumbs upon the ground.
   Birds need help in winter to eat,
   They depend on you for a treat.

2. Peanut butter and sunflow'r seeds,
   Popcorn balls, all make good bird feeds.
   Suet, birdseed, apples too
   Keep them living the whole year through.

Bird-Feeding Mobiles

Since many birds do not migrate south to warmer climates for the winter, they may need your help to survive especially when there's snow covering the ground.

The children may make bird-feeding mobiles using wire coat hangers and a variety of foods. Divide your class into groups of three or four to make these mobiles. They should be allowed to construct their mobiles in any combinations of available bird foods that they desire. Of course, you need to provide materials that will help them make creative mobiles. These materials could include wire hangers, string, clothespins, pipe cleaners, and small paper cups. Foods they may want to string for the birds to eat are Froot Loops™ or other round toasted cereals, popcorn (already popped), cranberries, dried fruits like raisins, colored marshmallows, and even small cubes of bread. Fruit skins can also be peeled in long pieces by the teacher to hang from the mobiles. Cut circles of bread and spread with butter or peanut butter and then sprinkle with sunflower seeds or other birdseeds. Paper cups could have peanut butter smeared on the outside surfaces and hung upside-down with popcorn (already popped) stuck all over them to form nutritious bells! When the mobiles are all decorated, each group should show their mobile to the rest of the class and then hang them in various places all over the school grounds. They don't have to be hung just in trees; they may be hung from fences and under eaves of the roof. Check daily to see how much of the food has been eaten. Collect the empty wire hangers and repeat the activity if the weather is still snowy and the birds are still needing food. Note which locations are the best feeding spots and hang more mobiles there.

All Night, All Day
African-American Spiritual

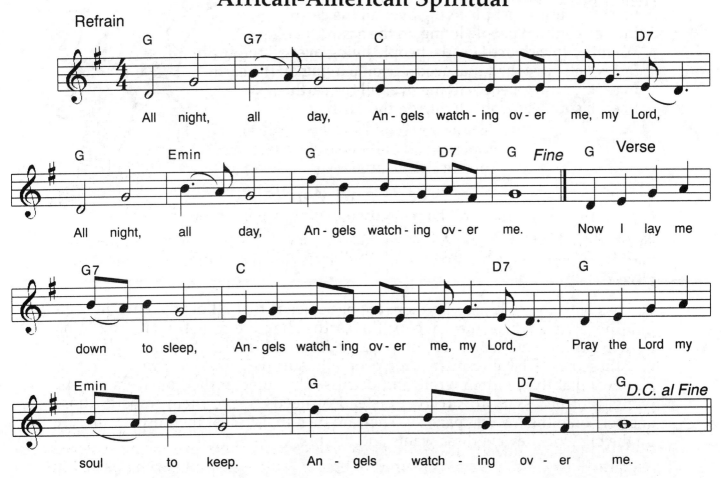

GA1522

Verse 2:

All night, all day, angels watching over me, my Lord,
All night, all day, angels watching over me.
If I die before I wake, angels watching over me, my Lord,
Pray the Lord my soul to take, angels watching over me.
All night, all day, angels watching over me, my Lord,
All night, all day, angels watching over me.

Here are two new verses sung to the tune of "All Night, All Day":

Snowflakes Dancing to the Earth

1. Lightly from the sky, snowflakes dancing softly to the earth,
   Lightly from the sky, snowflakes dancing to the earth.
   Each one's diff'rent, that's their fame,
   Snowflakes dancing softly to the earth.
   But to me they look the same,
   Snowflakes dancing to the earth.
   Lightly from the sky, snowflakes dancing softly to the earth,
   Lightly from the sky, snowflakes dancing to the earth.

2. In each country, people living over all the earth,
   In each country, people living on the earth.
   We differ like colored beads, people living over all the earth,
   But we all have the same needs, people living on the earth.
   In each country, people living over all the earth,
   In each country, people living on the earth.

Needs and Wants

Here is an exercise that will help children distinguish between needs and wants. Many children do not really distinguish between the two, and this can lead to unhappiness, bitterness, and other undesirable traits such as uncontrollable jealousy, selfishness, and greed.

Discuss with the children that there are basic needs that all people have in common no matter where they live on the earth. They are to list what they think these needs are on the big "N" on page 79. Be sure that the children understand that these needs have to be met for people to survive (air, food, water, shelter). Review what the children wrote and discuss why some of their answers may be wants (not necessary to survive) instead of needs. Have them transfer those answers onto the "W" on page 79. They are then to list what their own wants are on the big "W." Review these wants and discuss.

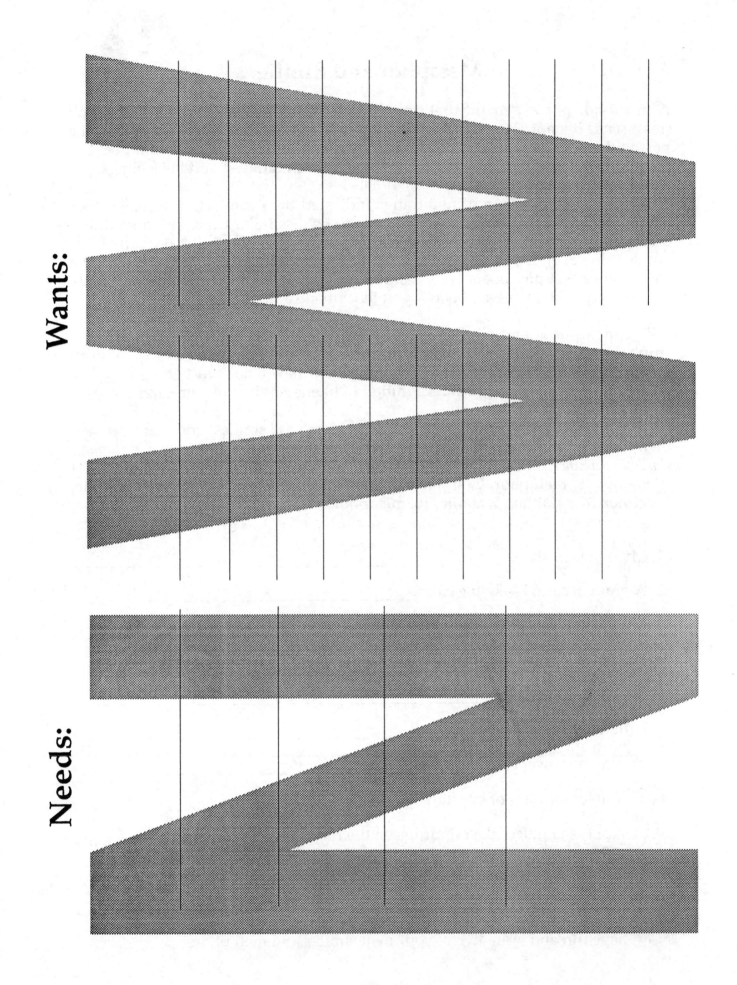

Wants:

Needs:

79

Metaphor and Simile

A metaphor is a statement that one thing is something else which in a literal (real) sense it's not. For example, "Oh, my love is a red, red rose." Obviously, the person the poet has written about is not literally a red, red rose. But that poet has compared his love to a red, red rose to better explain himself and his feelings.

A simile is a comparison of two things indicated by a connective word such as *like, as,* or *than.* The things compared have to be dissimilar (unalike) in kind. For example, "Your feet are like my mom's" is not a simile, but a literal (real) observation. However, if you were to say, "Your feet are like boats," you have used a simile since feet and boats are dissimilar. If you omit the connective word *like* and just say, " Your feet are boats," you have made a metaphor.

Using metaphors and similes in your writing for the sake of freshness and emphasis will make it much more colorful and interesting to the reader. You can notice similarities between two things that you never noticed before, and it is pleasurable to cause a sudden recognition of likenesses in a reader's mind.

Look at the sentences. Some are metaphors, some are similes, and some are neither. Decide what each sentence is and then write either the word *metaphor, simile,* or *neither* on the blank line by each sentence. (Answers for the teacher's eyes only: 1. metaphor, 2. simile, 3. simile, 4. metaphor, 5. neither, 6. simile, 7. neither, 8. metaphor, 9. simile, 10. metaphor.

1. My dog is a whale! _____

2. A grain of sand is like the earth._____

3. My Porsche flew like a speedy bullet. _____

4. His voice was the roar of a lion in a cage! _____

5. My chair is a rocker. _____

6. I am fatter than a ripe fruit. _____

7. The lawn mower cuts like a dull kitchen knife. _____

8. The table is a sheet of black ice. _____

9. His music sounded like raindrops on the roof. _____

10. The sun moving across the sky was a golden eye watching the earth.

_____

Now, have fun and write five of your own similes and metaphors!

GA1522

February

81

Fiddle-Dee-Dee
Folk Song from England

Fid-dle-dee-dee, Fid-dle-dee-dee, The fly has marr-ied the bum-ble-bee. Says the

fly, says he, "Will you mar-ry me, and live with me, sweet bum-ble-bee?"

Fid-dle-dee-dee, Fid-dle-dee-dee, The fly has mar-ried the bum-ble-bee.

Verse 2:

Fiddle-dee-dee, fiddle-dee-dee,
The fly has married the bumblebee.
Says the bee, says she, "I'll live under your wing,
And you'll never know that I carry a sting."
Fiddle-dee-dee, fiddle-dee-dee,
The fly has married the bumblebee.

Verse 3:

Fiddle-dee-dee, fiddle-dee-dee,
The fly has married the bumblebee.
So when the parson had joined the pair,
They both went out to take the air.
Fiddle-dee-dee, fiddle-dee-dee,
The fly has married the bumblebee.

Verse 4:

Fiddle-dee-dee, fiddle-dee-dee,
The fly has married the bumblebee.
And the flies did buzz and the bells did ring,
Did you ever hear so merry a thing?
Fiddle-dee-dee, fiddle-dee-dee,
The fly has married the bumblebee.

GA1522

Verse 5:

Fiddle-dee-dee, fiddle-dee-dee,
The fly has married the bumblebee.
And then to think that of all the flies,
The bumblebee should carry the prize.
Fiddle-dee-dee, fiddle-dee-dee,
The fly has married the bumblebee.

Here are three new verses sung to the tune of "Fiddle-Dee-Dee":

Valentine's Day

Valentine's Day! Valentine's Day!
A time to share and to give love away.
It's a day to show what is in your heart,
To show you care is the best part.
Valentine's Day! Valentine's Day!
A time to share and to give love away.

Valentine's Day! Valentine's Day!
A time to share and to give love away.
There are many different kinds of love,
For people you may be thinking of.
Valentine's Day! Valentine's Day!
A time to share and to give love away.

Valentine's Day! Valentine's Day!
A time to share and to give love away.
Make a card, give candy or flowers too,
So many ways to say, "I love you!"
Valentine's Day! Valentine's Day!
A time to share and to give love away.

GA1522

A Valentine for Me!

Create a valentine to yourself. Think of what you like about yourself and list these traits on this valentine. Qualities can be both physical appearance or personality traits. Color your valentine, cut it out, and place it where you can read it every day.

Love

There are many different types of love. These include romantic love, patriotism (love of country), love of God, love of animals, love for your parents and family, love for your friends, self-love, and love of inanimate objects or activities.

Complete this list. You don't have to fill all of the lines, but if you run out of room, use a separate sheet of paper.

People/Animals I Love	One Way I Show My Love for Each
1. _____	_____
2. _____	_____
3. _____	_____
4. _____	_____
5. _____	_____
6. _____	_____
7. _____	_____
8. _____	_____
9. _____	_____
10. _____	_____

Complete these sentences. You may choose to answer only some or all.

1. I love myself, and I show it by _____

_____

2. I love my country, and I show it by _____

_____

3. I love God, and I show it by _____

_____

4. I love_____, and I show it by _____
   (fill in activity or object)

_____

Now, show your love on Valentine's Day by making special valentines for one, several, or all of the people, animals, activities, or things appearing in the previous exercises. For example, a valentine to your dog could be some dog biscuits tied up with red bows and decorated with construction paper hearts. A valentine to baseball could be a poem written about the game and read to your classmates.

GA1522

Happy Are They
Israeli Round

Here is a new song sung to the tune of "Happy Are They":

Feelings

Feelings are constantly changing;
Emotions make us human.
Feelings are constantly changing;
Emotions make us human.
Laughing, crying, fearing, sighing, loving,
Anger, jealousy are natural emotions.
Feelings are constantly changing;
Emotions make us human.
Feelings are constantly changing;
Emotions make us human.

Here is a story to read. There will be something for you to do with the story after you have read it.

Chance's Angry Day

Chance felt just fine when he arrived at school. When he got to music class something happened (1) <u>that changed his whole day</u>. The music teacher picked five different rhythm instruments for the children to play to accompany a song they'd learned. The children were taking turns playing the instruments in groups of five. When it was Chance's turn to choose an instrument, another child had already chosen the big conga drum that Chance had his heart set on playing. There was a tambourine that was left to play so Chance picked up the tambourine, threw it on the floor, stomped back to his seat, and refused to play at all. He was very angry.

When Chance went back to his homeroom, (2) he was still angry and refused to do his work. His homeroom teacher looked at his paper and remarked that (3) since he did not do his work, he'd have to work on it tonight at home.

After class, Chance went to lunch and, while waiting in line, he kept thinking about what his homeroom teacher had told him. The more he thought about it, the more it affected his appetite, and he (4) only picked at his food causing most of it to be thrown away.

At recess, Chance felt (5) so angry that he took the basketball and threw it directly at a little girl in his class.

Later in the day during library class, Chance was (6) still angry, and instead of reading silently, he tore a page out of his book and threw it at another student. The librarian told him (7) to go to the principal's office.

The principal read the librarian's note while Chance sat in his office. The principal felt the only thing for him to do was (8) call Chance's parents and make them pay for the book. This is the end of the story.

Chance's day was what he made it. Whatever happened was a reaction to the emotions and attitudes he carried with him all day. Have you ever had a day like that? You can help Chance change the outcome of his day. Look at the numbered and underlined passages in the story and rewrite them to make Chance's day more positive. How might his day have been totally different if he'd not carried his anger with him after the incident in music class? For instance, number 1 might be changed to read " . . . that made him angry, but he forgot about it when music class was over."

Here are some sample answers for the teacher's eyes only. Feel free to have the children think of their own answers. These are given only as a guide to help the children should they get stuck on an answer. There really are no right answers.

2. " . . . he forgot his anger and set about doing his work."
3. " . . . Chance's work looked very good and seemed to be improving every day."
4. " . . . ate everything on his plate."
5. " . . . so happy that he played basketball with all of his friends without once getting into an argument."
6. " . . . reading silently when the librarian came and looked over his shoulder."
7. " . . . he'd read more biographies than anyone else and to take a note about this to the principal's office."
8. " . . . congratulate Chance and reward him with a gift certificate for another book."

Wild Bird
Singing Game from Japan

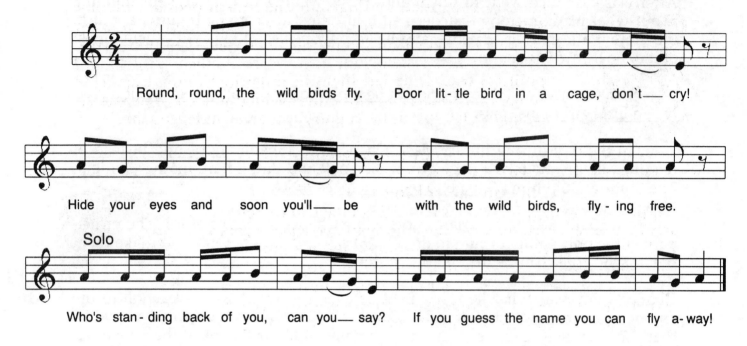

Round, round, the wild birds fly. Poor lit-tle bird in a cage, don't— cry!

Hide your eyes and soon you'll— be with the wild birds, fly-ing free.

Solo

Who's stan-ding back of you, can you— say? If you guess the name you can fly a-way!

Here is another verse sung to the tune of "Wild Bird."

World Leaders

World leaders peacefully work to make changes so people live free.
Gandhi, King, Mandela, too, knew that change was overdue.
They were important men; they led the way.
Leaders like these are needed to this day.

Important World Leaders

Divide your class into three groups that are as equal as possible. Each group will need to read and study one particular leader. After they've read one of the following paragraphs that tells about their leader, the teacher will read statements. The students will hold up their hands when a statement has to do with their leader. In most cases, the statements will have to do with more than one of these men. Even though they lived in different time periods, the similarities will be fairly obvious.

Copy for one group.

Mahatma Gandhi

Mahatma Gandhi was born in India in 1869 which is when the country was ruled by England. The Indian people were not able to elect their own leaders or to make their own laws. Gandhi knew that for his people to be free, they must work peacefully and patiently for many years. As their spiritual and political leader, he led them in resisting domination. This sometimes resulted in authorities jailing him. He was assassinated in 1948, just as his country was given independence.

Copy for one group.

Martin Luther King, Jr.

Martin Luther King, Jr., was born in 1929 in the United States at a time when African Americans did not have equal rights with white Americans. After becoming a Baptist minister, King and his followers resisted unequal practices against African Americans peacefully for many years until they were treated the same. King was put in jail by authorities on several occasions. He was assassinated in 1968.

Copy for one group.

Nelson Mandela

Nelson Mandela was born in 1918 in South Africa. He grew up under a system called apartheid which means that black South Africans and white South Africans cannot live together in the same areas or work equally at the same jobs. Since his early twenties, Mandela has worked for equal rights which resulted in his spending twenty-eight years of his life in prison. Ever since his release from prison in 1990, he has continued to work for a South Africa that can live in peace with equal rights for blacks and whites.

Read these statements to your whole class. They are to raise their hands if a statement applies to the leader that they've read about. Many of these statements will apply to more than one leader. If they apply to only one or two, be sure to point out to the children who the statement is about so that they will learn something about all three important world leaders.

1. I was born in a time when my people were being treated unfairly. (All 3)
2. I worked for many years to bring about change. (All 3)
3. I was assassinated. (Gandhi, King)
4. Because of my activities to bring about change, I was jailed by authorities. (All 3)
5. I used peaceful methods to bring increased freedom to my people. (All 3)
6. I was a Baptist minister. (King)

Don Gato
Folk Song from Mexico

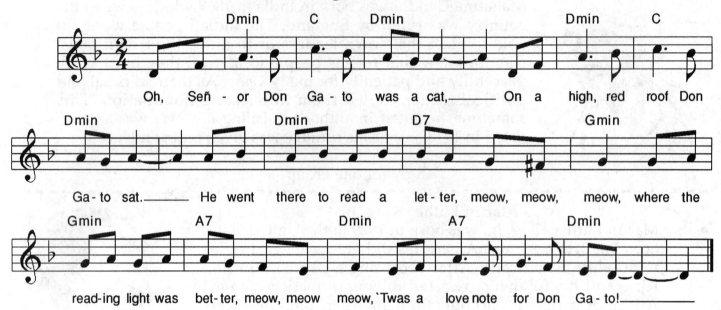

Oh, Señ - or Don Ga - to was a cat,——— On a high, red roof Don Ga - to sat.——— He went there to read a let - ter, meow, meow, meow, where the

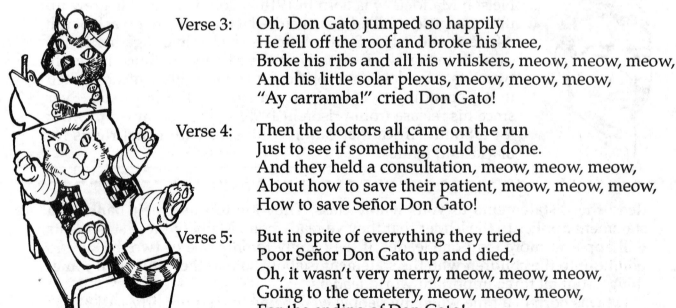

read-ing light was bet- ter, meow, meow meow, `Twas a love note for Don Ga- to!———

Verse 2: "I adore you!" wrote the lady cat,
Who was fluffy, white, and nice and fat.
There was not a sweeter kitty, meow, meow, meow,
In the country or the city, meow, meow, meow,
And she said she'd wed Don Gato!

Verse 3: Oh, Don Gato jumped so happily
He fell off the roof and broke his knee,
Broke his ribs and all his whiskers, meow, meow, meow,
And his little solar plexus, meow, meow, meow,
"Ay carramba!" cried Don Gato!

Verse 4: Then the doctors all came on the run
Just to see if something could be done.
And they held a consultation, meow, meow, meow,
About how to save their patient, meow, meow, meow,
How to save Señor Don Gato!

Verse 5: But in spite of everything they tried
Poor Señor Don Gato up and died,
Oh, it wasn't very merry, meow, meow, meow,
Going to the cemetery, meow, meow, meow,
For the ending of Don Gato!

Verse 6: When the funeral passed the market square
Such a smell of fish was in the air,
Though his burial was slated, meow, meow, meow,
He became reanimated, meow, meow, meow,
He came back to life, Don Gato!

Here's a new verse for the tune of "Don Gato":

Release It
Let your anger out creatively,
Write a poem instead of hitting me.
Write a song or draw a picture; don't delay!
Feel your anger and frustration fade away.
It's the best way to release it!

Emotional Creativity Webs

Too many times, it is assumed that one has to be in a good or happy mood to do a creative activity. This is not necessarily so. Children many times have no recognizable or acceptable outlet for negative emotions. Therefore, they may lash out in anger or frustration at another child by hitting or throwing something. Or they may throw temper tantrums or bottle their feelings up inside. They should be encouraged to express themselves with the arts no matter what their emotions. Anger or sadness should be placed openly into art forms such as finger painting; painting with a brush; modeling clay; writing a poem, story, song, or play; or taking photographs. Other children will recognize some of their own emotions in the words of their peers. And this will teach them that expressing yourself through an art form is an acceptable way of expressing negative emotions. Have the children either tell or write down a list of things that connect with the word *angry* using the word web form. Put the word *angry* in the middle of a page and let them tell you to write down or write down themselves other words branching from that word. Other words to use to start a word web could

GA1522

be *sadness, jealousy, frustration*. Each child's word web will look different. After they've completed their word webs, they will use them as the basis for an art project. They may use the words in their web to create a poem, picture, story, play, or photograph.

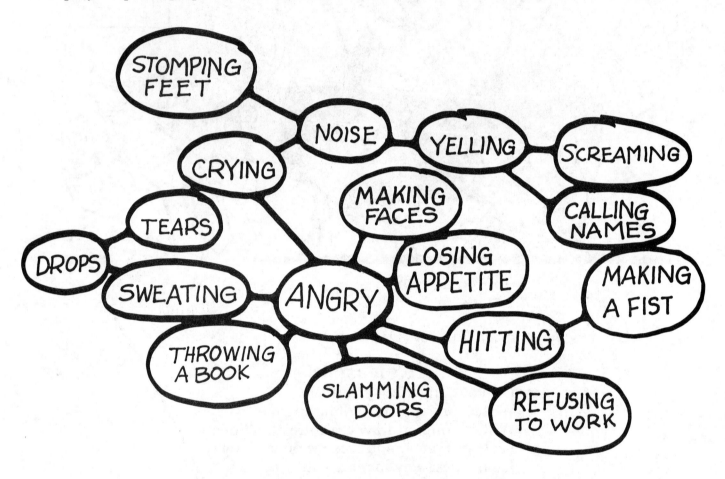

This poem was composed using the words from this web.

Angry Poem

I wanted to hit you for what you said,
Or throw a book right at your head!
I wanted to call you all kinds of bad names,
And exclude you from all of our playground games.
I wanted to hurt you for what you said,
But I wrote a word web and poem instead,
For poems are better than making noise,
Or crying tears, or slamming doors.
I'd just get in trouble for making a fist,
I feel so much better just making a list.
And when you are sorry for causing me pain,
I hope you'll tell me, and we'll be friends again.

March

93

GA1522

Cherry Blooms
Japanese Folk Song

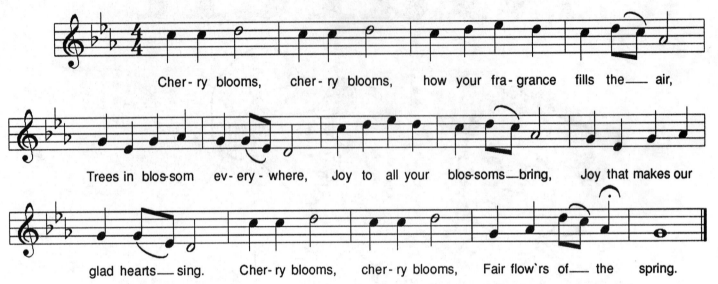

Cher-ry blooms, cher-ry blooms, how your fra-grance fills the— air, Trees in blos-som ev-ery-where, Joy to all your blos-soms—bring, Joy that makes our glad hearts— sing. Cher-ry blooms, cher-ry blooms, Fair flow'rs of— the spring.

Verse 2:

> Cherry blooms, cherry blooms,
> Spread your perfume all around,
> Over country, over town,
> Ev'rywhere is beauty rare,
> Joy you bring for all to share,
> Cherry blooms, cherry blooms,
> Fair flow'rs of the spring.

Here is another verse sung to the tune of "Cherry Blooms":

Fair Flowers

> Hyacinth, daffodil, buttercup, and crocus small,
> Peony and iris tall,
> Honeysuckle, begonia,
> Poppy, daisy, azalea,
> Roses red, pink, and white,
> Fair flow'rs of the spring.

Bulletin Board Bees

Discuss with the children how bees help flowers reproduce by spreading pollen from flower to flower, carrying bits of pollen on their legs and bodies. Friendships can grow and bloom like flowers, but they must have some help from the right types of "be's." People must carry certain qualities and attitudes into a friendship. Children can create a springtime bulletin board with this in mind that will form a garden of flowers and bees. Use the pattern of the bee and flower. Each child will have at least one bee and flower to color and cut out. Each is to

GA1522

put a descriptive word in the center of the flower that tells a way to "be" in order to help friendships grow. For instance, "Be kind," "Be compassionate," "Be courteous" will all help friendships grow. Have the children think of as many different descriptive ways to "be" as possible. Challenge them to each think of a word that nobody else has used. Be sure the children are aware that this "be" is a homophone, and that the insect is spelled "bee." Once each child has finished coloring, cutting out, and writing the descriptive word on the flower, mount it on a bulletin board. Title the overall board "Seeds You Sow Help Friendship Grow."

GA1522

Parts of a Flower

There are four main parts to a flower. In the example below color the four different parts with four different colors. Later, on a separate sheet of paper, design and color your own flower. Be sure you include and label all four parts of the flower.

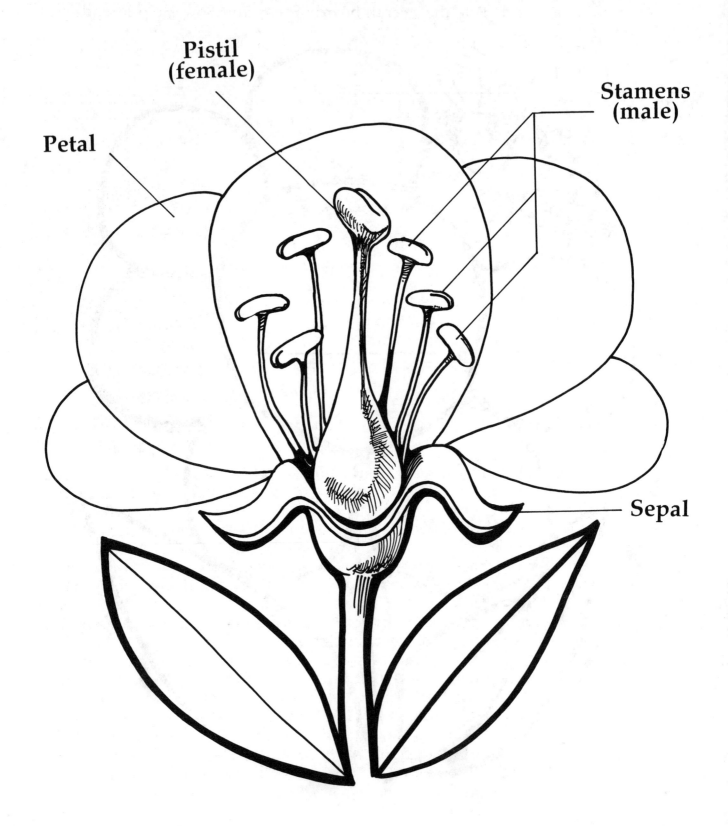

Pistil
(female)

Stamens
(male)

Petal

Sepal

96

Cucu
Vietnamese Folk Song

Blue - birds sing, "Cu - Cu."   **Red** - birds sing, "Cu - Cu."

Black - birds sing, "Cu - Cu."   **All** birds sing, "Cu - Cu."

Here are two new verses sung to the tune of "Cucu":

Pantomime

1. When we pantomime we don't make a sound.
   When we pantomime we can move around.

2. When we pantomime we like to pretend.
   When we pantomime we can imagine.

Pantomimes

Pantomime was actually practiced as an art beginning in ancient Rome. In those days, one actor would play all of the parts without speaking a word, but with music and singing in the background as an accompaniment. People who pantomime must use their imaginations to create images in the viewers' minds. Let various members of the class pantomime by drawing one of the categories listed on page 98. Cut out the little squares with categories listed on them and put them in a box. When students see what category they've drawn, they may choose a specific activity or item to pantomime. Put the category card back in the box so that it may be drawn again by someone else. If someone else happens to draw that same category, a different activity or item in that category must be pantomimed. The rest of the class will be allowed to know what the category is and will guess what the specific activity or item is that is being pantomimed. Before a student begins the pantomime, he or she must whisper to the teacher what it is he or she will be acting out. The class gets one minute to guess the answer. When the teacher hears the correct answer, he or she points at the child who guessed correctly, and that child gets to be the next mime. If that child has already had a turn to be the mime, he or she will get to choose someone who hasn't had a turn.

GA1522

Pantomime Categories

Cut these out and place in a box for students to draw. Feel free to add more categories on small slips of paper.

Farm Animals	Sports/Sports Equipment
Weather Conditions	Fairy Tales/Nursery Rhymes
Songs	Furniture
Careers/Occupations	Vehicles
Movies	Books
School Subjects	Foods
Insects	Musical Instruments
Tools	Circus Acts

The Wind Blew East
Bahamian Folk Song

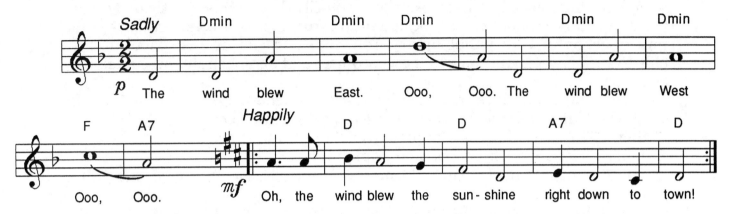

The wind blew East. Ooo, Ooo. The wind blew West Ooo, Ooo. Oh, the wind blew the sun-shine right down to town!

Here is another verse sung to the tune of "The Wind Blew East":

Some Sounds Are . . .

1. Some sounds are soft ooo ooo,
   Some sounds are sad ooo ooo,
   But the sounds I like best are loud and glad,
   But the sounds I like best are loud and glad!

2. Some sounds are high ooo ooo,
   Some sounds are low ooo ooo,
   And the sounds travel faster than winds can blow,
   And the sounds travel faster than winds can blow!

3. Some sounds take time ooo ooo,
   They're very long ooo ooo,
   But some sounds are quite short like part of this song,
   But some sounds are quite short like part of this song!

Sound Bounds

Sounds have many different qualities. Children may experiment with loud and soft sounds by doing the following activity. Take an empty metal container with a plastic lid that is removable (like mixed nuts come in). Tell the children that they are going to try out a bunch of different items in the container to measure how loud or soft the sounds are. Put in cut-up straw pieces, close the lid, and let one child shake the container. Then have all the children decide if the sound was loud or soft. Do this with each item listed and record which items are loud, soft, or both. The children will discover that some items are only loud, some are only soft (like the cut-up straws), and some can be both loud and soft according to how the container is shaken. The children may want to guess whether what they're putting into the container will be loud or soft before they try it.

Items to test include confetti, dried pasta, metal screws, leaves, gravel, sand, candy hearts, cut-up straws, beans, rice, small seeds, chalk pieces, rabbit food pellets, and any other items the children may bring from home to try.

GA1522

Sounds of Music

To demonstrate the concepts of sound related in the new version of the song, play the children some musical examples that clearly demonstrate them. Most of these musical examples can be located on records, tapes, or compact discs in the music section of your public library. Your music teacher in the school may be able to supply you with some of these or others that demonstrate these qualities.

Fast: "Russian Dance" from *The Nutcracker* by Tchaikovsky
Slow: "Arabian Dance" from *The Nutcracker* by Tchaikovsky
Soft: "In the Hall of the Mountain King" (beginning part) by Grieg
Loud: "Hoedown" from *Rodeo* by Copland
High: "Ballet of the Unhatched Chicks" from *Pictures at an Exhibition* by Mussorgsky
Low: "Jimbo's Lullaby" from *Children's Corner Suite* by Debussy
Sad: *Adagio for Strings* by Barber
Glad: "The Stars and Stripes Forever" by Sousa

Let the children also bring examples of their own from home. Play a part of each example and decide as a class what qualities of sound are represented.

GA1522

The Shapes and Colors of Sound

Play an example of each expressive quality of music (soft, loud, fast, slow, high, low, sad, and glad) and make sure each student has a copy of this page. Have students write in the box the expressive quality it makes them think of and then color how it feels to them.

Copy for the students.

From the expressive qualities of music that have been studied, draw your own shape to illustrate one of these expressive qualities. Color it appropriately too. Display these shapes and let the class members guess which quality each one illustrates.

Sound Statements

Complete the following statements by choosing one of these expressive qualities to fill in the blank: soft, loud, high, low, fast, slow, sad, glad. This is an open-ended exercise allowing for discussion. There are no correct answers since each statement could be answered with one of several qualities of expression.

1. When a band marches by at a parade, I would expect to hear music that is
_____.

2. While sitting at a funeral, I heard music played that was_____.

3. At a wedding I would expect to hear_____ music.

4. When my mother rocks my baby sister to sleep, she sings a song that is
_____.

5. If I were to go to a dance, I would dance to music that was_____.

6. If I heard a piccolo player, I would expect the music to sound_____.

7. When the music box winds down, I would expect the music to sound
_____.

8. If I heard a bass guitar, the music would sound_____.

GA1522

103

GA1522

Keep in the Middle of the Road
African-American Spiritual

Verse 2:
I have no time to stop an' talk,
Keep in the middle of the road,
'Cause the road is rough an' it's hard to walk,
Keep in the middle of the road.
Gonna fix my eyes on the golden stair,
Gonna keep on a-goin' 'til I get there,
For my head is bound that crown for to wear,
Keep in the middle of the road.
Refrain

Verse 3:
The world is full of sinful things,
Keep in the middle of the road,
When your feet get tired put on your wings,
Keep in the middle of the road.
When you lay down in that road to die,
Watch them angels in the sky,
Put on your wings and get up an' fly,
Keep in the middle of the road.
Refrain

Here are three new verses sung to the tune of "Keep in the Middle of the Road":

I'm Growing Vegetables to Eat

Verse 1:
When Springtime sun comes bursting through,
I'm growing vegetables to eat,
I know just exactly what I must do,
I'm growing vegetables to eat.
I will get my rake and get my hoe,
And some bags of seeds that I can sow,
And I'll plant them neatly row by row,
I'm growing vegetables to eat.

Refrain:
I'm growing vegetables to eat,
Growing vegetables to eat,
There are beans to the right and potatoes to the left,
'Cause I'm growing vegetables to eat!

Verse 2:
When springtime rains come pouring down,
I'm growing vegetables to eat,
Showers help the seeds sprout from the ground,
I'm growing vegetables to eat.
Some are red and yellow, some are orange and green,
And they bounce the light with a shiny gleam,
The most colorful garden that I've ever seen!
I'm growing vegetables to eat.

Refrain:
I'm growing vegetables to eat,
Growing vegetables to eat,
There is squash to the right, and peppers to the left,
'Cause I'm growing vegetables to eat!

GA1522

Verse 3:
I'll tend my garden with great care,
I'm growing vegetables to eat,
Mother Nature has good things to share,
I'm growing vegetables to eat.
As I watch my plants grow tall and wide,
Being partners with nature gives me such great pride,
And I get a warm feeling deep down inside,
I'm growing vegetables to eat.

Refrain:
I'm growing vegetables to eat,
There are peas to the right and carrots to the left,
'Cause I'm growing vegetables to eat!

Hidden Vegetable Patch

Look for the names of these dozen vegetables in this hidden vegetable patch. Draw a rectangle around them when you find them. The vegetables you're looking for are broccoli, corn, squash, carrots, lettuce, onions, peppers, beans, potatoes, peas, celery, and cabbage.

```
A B Q M O N I O N S K R P G V J E D S Y
E R W J K N R F Y N P O U E C R B D E S
L O Q J N G W L X B O U J P E P P E R S
Y C E Q U M Z A Q G U O P W L R A Q W E
U C I J N M O P T W R E H P E G M P L Q
E O R H C A R R O T S U K L R E Y L Y H
U L R M B X Z X D R U O P Q Y G T E E W
Y I E W C X Z Y U Q D J K L P O I T R R
Q H B N M K J H G F T U E P R H W T Y L
W U G H J K L P O I U Y T R E W Q U Z S
C J V B N M P L J H C O R N R T Y C E Q
I E Q E R E W O E R T Y U I O P A E S U
O W A S D F G H T H H E H J K L P O I A
E N W B E A N S R A Y U I H N B G V M S
E P I J K I I O L G T C A B B A G E Q H
L Q R T U Y A Q V G Y O H J K L O P T E
U M E W P T G H J B V B E H J O P M N C
U E T K E E U I O E T L P S O N M D C S
O X W O A W L A X Y Z S Q U I S H W I H
Q U K M S H L K I N G V C P R T E D S Q
```

GA1522

My Colorful Vegetable Garden

Imagine that you're planting a vegetable garden that will be as colorful as possible. After each color listed, name at least one vegetable that is that color. The skin may be that color or the inside of the vegetable may be that color. See how many you can list for each color. Some may fit in several categories.

Red:_____

Orange:_____

Yellow: _____

Green: _____

Purple: _____

White: _____

Brown: _____

- -

(Answer key for the teacher's eyes only: Red: radishes, peppers, beets, rhubarb; Orange: carrots, yams/sweet potatoes; Yellow: corn, onions, peppers, squash; Green: broccoli, lettuce, beans, celery, cabbage, peas, peppers, zucchini, cucumbers; Purple: eggplant, onions; White: onions, cauliflower, potatoes, bok choy, zucchini [inside]; Brown: outside of potato.
This is by no means a comprehensive list. The children may think of other answers that apply.)

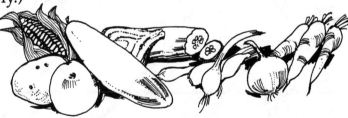

How Do Your Hybrids Grow?

Pretend that you are an experimental gardener who's blending together different kinds of vegetables to come up with something completely new. That means that you must also name your new creations by combining their two individual names into one. For instance, broccoli and cauliflower have been combined to produce a hybrid vegetable called a broccoflower. What would you name these hybrids? There are no correct answers. Be creative and use your own imagination!

1. lettuce + cabbage = _____

2. carrots + celery = _____

3. peas + cucumbers = _____

4. peppers + squash = _____

5. rhubarb + zucchini = _____

Use these spaces to think of your very own hybrids and their names. Then draw and color pictures of your hybrids and label them.

6. _____ + _____ = _____

7. _____ + _____ = _____

8. _____ + _____ = _____

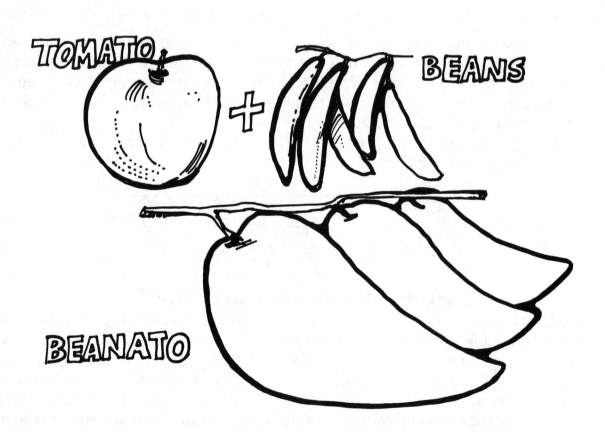

TOMATO + BEANS

BEANATO

April

109

The Flower
Singing Game from Puerto Rico

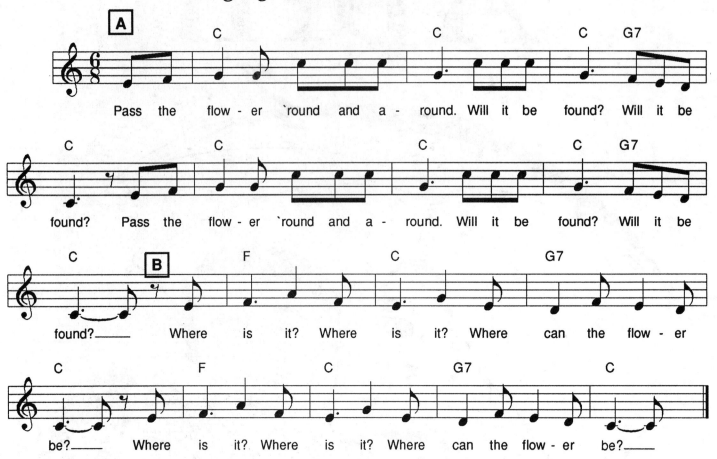

Pass the flow-er 'round and a-round. Will it be found? Will it be
found? Pass the flow-er 'round and a-round. Will it be found? Will it be
found?____ Where is it? Where is it? Where can the flow-er
be?____ Where is it? Where is it? Where can the flow-er be?____

Here is a new version sung to the tune of "The Flower":

Recycle

Use it once and use it again,
Recycle plastic, paper, and cans.
Collect glass and take it to town;
You can recycle green, clear, and brown.
Recycle, recycle, it's up to you and me.
Recycle, recycle, it's up to you and me.

Recycling Trek

Discuss with your class that space is running out in America to dump our trash
and garbage. Landfills are quickly filling up, and we are discovering long-term
ill effects from this disposal method. Much of what is thrown away could be
recycled if people were willing to take the trouble. Here is an activity for the
class to do to help in the recycling effort.

GA1522

Phase 1:  Contact your local recycling center or processor to arrange a field trip for your class to see exactly what materials are being recycled in quantity in your area (glass, paper, tin cans, plastic, aluminum cans, etc.). If a field trip is not possible, find out by phone what is being recycled and what preparations of the recycled materials are required. For instance, must aluminum cans be flattened; must bottle caps and plastic rings be removed from bottles, etc.? The class should be made aware of what materials are recyclable by the field trip or by class discussion.

Phase 2:  Discuss and vote on what material(s) the class would like to collect for recycling during the last two months of school. The decision will have to be made on where to store what is brought in for recycling. There are several options. One option is for the teacher to designate a certain day of the week as the day everyone brings what has been collected at home. Then after school, the teacher or a parent volunteer takes it to the recycling center and cashes it in. Another option is for the children to bring their recycled material(s) to a certain student's garage for storage. (If storing papers, avoid any fire hazards.) Then on a designated day all of the collected stuff could be taken by parent volunteers to the recycling center and cashed in. Hopefully each class will be able to find a plan that works well for them and their situation.

Phase 3:  Target a business in an area close to the school that has a recycling problem. The children may already be aware of many such businesses. For instance, a local convenience store may be discarding their empty aluminum cans and glass soda bottles with their regular trash. If their customers had an alternate container for these recyclables, the business might get in the habit of recycling. Other possible target businesses are restaurants, fast food places, or offices. After a target business has been chosen, the teacher should approach the owner or manager with a recycling proposal. The proposal would be that the class would like to provide their employees and/or customers the opportunity to recycle the targeted items (aluminum cans) by providing them with a free receptacle. Explain that the class has been recycling to save enough money to buy and decorate this receptacle for their business. Provide the business with the information about where to take the recycled items. Have more than one targeted business just in case you have to go to several before being accepted.

Phase 4:  With the money that has been earned by the class's recycling, discuss what type of recycling receptacle to purchase. Discuss the possibilities of decorating this receptacle. The decorations should encourage others to use the receptacle and should have which class donated it somewhere on it. It could also have a statement about why it's necessary or important to recycle. For instance, "Recycle your papers and save trees!" could be on the receptacle somewhere. Receptacles don't necessarily have to be large trash cans. Explore the different possibilities for receptacles with your class. A receptacle could be a large mesh laundry bag that hangs from a hook on the wall or a large cardboard box.

 GA1522

The children will be proud of themselves for initiating a good habit that hopefully the business will carry on. And they will have done something to make a difference in their own community.

One More Time

Recycling possibilities are around you all the time. One agency that quite often needs help with using recycled materials is the local animal shelter. Many are in need of short, flat cardboard boxes that cases of pop are delivered in. They use these for disposable cat litter boxes. Rather than the boxes being just thrown away, they could serve an important function one more time before being thrown away or recycled. This prolongs the life of the cardboard box and helps the animal shelter at the same time. As a class project, arrange for the students to collect these cardboard boxes from grocery and convenience stores on a regular basis. Then deliver them to the animal shelter on a regular basis if the shelter will use or already is using this litter box method. Think of other things that can be used in a different way for one more time.

"Use it up, wear it out, make it do, do without!"

GA1522

Did You Ever See a Lassie?
Traditional Scottish Tune

Did you ev - er see a {las - sie, a {las - sie a {las - sie, Did you
{lad - die,} {lad - die} {lad - die,}

ev - er see a {las - sie} go this way and that? Go this way and that way, and
{lad - die}

this way and that way. Did you ev - er see a {las - sie} go this way and that?
{lad - die}

Here is a new version sung to the tune of "Did You Ever See a Lassie?":

Oh, We're Going to Have an Earth Day
Oh, we're going to have an Earth Day, an Earth Day, an Earth Day,
Oh, we're going to have an Earth Day when April comes 'round!
But Earth Day is each day,
We'll all help in some way,
Oh, we're going to have an Earth Day when April comes 'round!

113

GA1522

Earth Day Game Fest!

While Earth Day traditionally concentrates on environmental concerns, it is also a good idea to simply become familiar with how people in other countries and cultures have fun. Besides, Earth Day should really be every day, not just once a year! To celebrate Earth Day, plan to have not only exercises that educate about problems that must be solved with our environment, but also remember to have a game fest using games from all over the earth. The six games included here can help children become more aware that children all over our earth are alike in that they like to play and have fun.

African: "Jarabadach"

This African game seems somewhat close to tic-tac-toe, but it is actually a bit trickier. Only two players at a time can play this game, with one player having three white stones (or whatever markers you choose) and the other player having three black stones (markers). The diagram pictured on this page can be dug with a stick into the ground outside (like they do in Africa) or marked on paper to play inside. Notice that the large rectangle is divided into four small rectangles by two lines. The numbers show that there are nine points of the large rectangle that the plays are made on. By taking turns a player may put one stone on any of the nine points of the diagram. The whole idea is to get three in a row before your opponent can. Of course, all six pieces can be placed without getting three in a row. Players then take turns in moving along the lines one space at a time until one of the players wins the game.

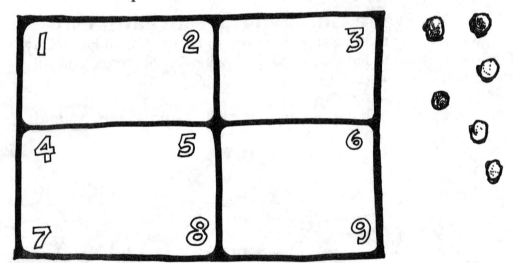

African: "Nsikwi"

Two players are involved. They sit on the ground facing each other at least three yards (2.75 meters) apart. Africans use a piece of corncob about three inches high (7.5 cm) to set in front of each player. It is probably more convenient to use small plastic bottles or other lightweight items to substitute for the corncobs. After the start of the game is signaled, each player rolls a small ball across the distance trying to knock down the opponent's corncob or plastic bottle. Every time the bottle is knocked over, a point is scored. Set a goal of points to be reached, and the first player to reach that goal will be declared the winner.

Brazilian: **"Morral"**

This game is a variation of an old game called Grab Bag. Each child brings a gift which may be comical or quite inexpensive. A large sack or box is filled with the gifts. Make sure enough gifts are in the container so there's one for each child. Write on slips of paper a suggested stunt to be performed. Each child gets a chance to draw a slip and then entertain the rest of the class by performing the stunt the slip directs. After performing, he or she gets to grab a prize from the other container. Give everyone a turn. Here are some suggested stunts:

Say rapidly seven times, "Toy boat."
Balance a piece of chalk on your nose.
Put one hand where the other hand cannot touch it.
Bark like a small dog and then like a large dog.
Imitate a pirate by saying, "Avast, me hardies!"
Dance around the room three times with a meter- or yardstick for a partner.
Say three nice things about someone in the room while standing on one leg.
In Pig Latin say, "Four score and seven years ago."
Rearrange the letters in your last name to come up with a new name.
Pretend to be a butterfly that flies around the room.
Imitate a police officer directing traffic at an intersection.
Pose as Napoleon.
Imitate an old woman calling her cat.
Sing the song, "Did You Ever See a Lassie?"
Duck walk from the front of the room back to your seat.

Let the children add more stunts to this list. They should write their stunts on slips of paper. The teacher should look over what they've written before adding them to the game. Some of the stunts might involve something that could be done on Earth Day to help the planet.

Chinese: **"Lame Chicken"**

This game is somewhat like Hopscotch. Begin with ten sticks that are all about one foot long (30.5 cm) and arranged in a row like rungs on a ladder. The spaces between the rungs are 10 inches (25.5 cm). Hopping on only one foot like a lame chicken, the player tries to hop over these sticks without touching any of them since to do so will disqualify him or her. The player gets just one hop between sticks. If the player manages to hop over the last stick, he or she must reach down and pick it up while still balancing on one foot and then hop back over the remaining sticks to where he or she began. After dropping the stick, he or she then hops back over the nine remaining sticks to pick up the ninth stick in the same manner as before. This goes on until all of the sticks have been picked up and returned to the starting point. Disqualification occurs if both of the player's feet touch the ground or if a stick is touched with a foot.

Chinese: "Pickup Race"

This game is similar to the egg in the spoon race except each player receives a pair of chopsticks and two bowls. The bowls are placed nine feet (2.75 meters) apart. Five marbles (or marshmallows, nuts, popped popcorn, small wrapped candies) are placed in the bowls for each player on one side of the room. When the signal to go is given, players must pick up their marbles (or other items) one at a time with their chopsticks and carry them one at a time the distance to the other bowl. Whoever transfers all five marbles (items) from one bowl to the other first wins the game. At no time are the hands of players allowed to touch the marbles (items). If a marble (item) is dropped, a player must pick it up with the chopsticks and return it to the original bowl before starting again.

Danish: "Fishing Game"

Assuming that each child has a 12-inch (30.5-cm) ruler, have each of them tape a length of heavy thread about seven inches (18 cm) long to the end of it. On the other end of the thread, tie a dress hook. This will serve as each child's fishing pole. The fish can be made from corks into which staples are driven into the larger upper surface. Each fish has a number from 1 to 20 written in ink on the bottom. Corks or "fish" can be painted to add color. All the fish are placed on a tabletop instead of floated on water. Allowing only four players at a time, the fishing commences with children catching the dress hook on the end of the fishing pole into the staple on the fish. Players must unhook their fish as soon as caught and then go after another. After all of the fish have been caught, add the numbers from the bottom of each cork to determine who has caught the most pounds of fish and thus wins the game. The excitement can be quite funny when there's only one fish left on the table!

Older children may want to make the game pieces and invite a class of younger children in to play the games to celebrate Earth Day. Each older child could be paired with a younger child to help that child with the games. Everyone could take turns playing the games so that each child has a chance to try each game.

GA1522

Lotus Blossoms
Chinese Folk Song

Smoothly flowing

Here I bring you sweet scen-ted flow'rs Sweet are they from

dew - y bow'rs; Per-fume light as sum-mer air, Fra-grant flow'rs, of our

friend - ship true. These I bring to you from my bow'r bloom-ing fair,

Fra - grant flow'rs of our friend - ship true.

Here is a new version sung to the tune of "Lotus Blossoms":

Kites

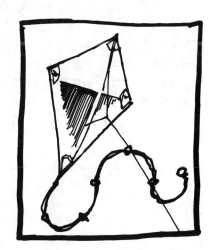

Kites of all colors floating high in the air,
Wind currents keep them suspended up there.
Watch the kites riding on the breeze.
Kites are our dreams hov'ring just out of reach.
Paper, wood, and strings floating above the trees.
Kites are our dreams hov'ring just out of reach.

Kite of Dreams

Kites are like dreams because they float out of our reach. But just like kites, dreams can be connected to us by a string. That string can be used to allow the dreams to happen and to allow the kite to fly. String can also reel the dreams in for us and make them down to earth.

GA1522

What design or picture would you draw on your "Kite of Dreams"? And what do you think the string will be made of to make those dreams come true?

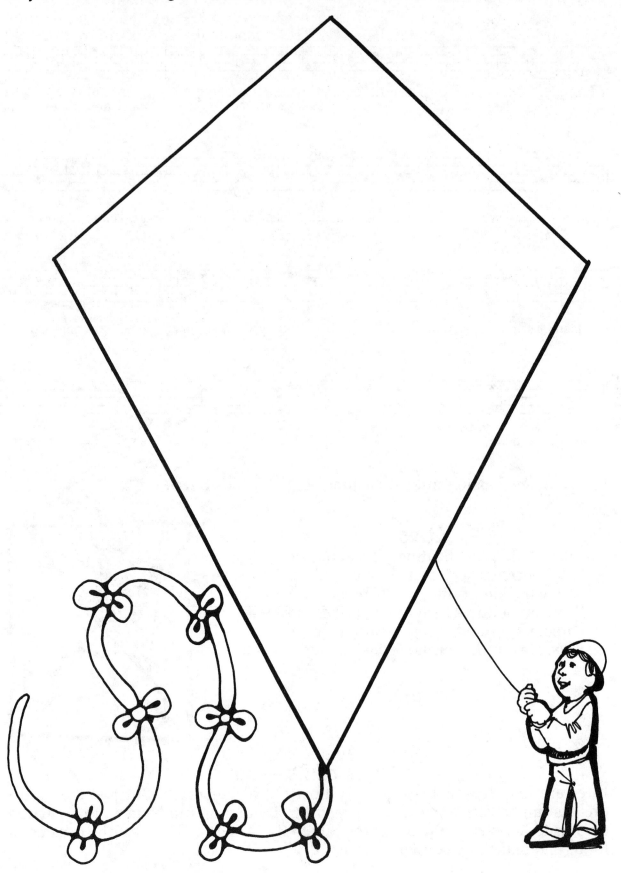

Kite Rhymes to Make a Poem Fly

For many kites to fly, they have to have a tail. Sometimes rhyming words are used for a poem to fly in the mind of the reader. Have the children name as many words as they can think of that rhyme with the word *kite*. Write them on the board as they name them. Then each child may make up a poem by choosing from the words on the board. Poems may be as short or as long as students like. Share the poems with the class by reading them aloud. Have them write their poems on pieces of paper cut to resemble a kite. Display these on a bulletin board titled "Kite Tales."

Kite Tails

Many things have tails. Look at the pictures and color any that have tails.

GA1522

Breezes Are Blowing
Luiseño Indian Rain Chant

Breez-es are blow-ing, Blow-ing clouds of wat-er; Breez-es are blow-ing,

Blow-ing clouds of wat-er; On my face, rain-ing, Rain-ing from the o-cean;

Breez-es are blow-ing, Blow-ing clouds of wat-er.

Here are two more verses sung to the tune of "Breezes Are Blowing":

Raindrops Are Falling

1. Raindrops are falling and the earth is drinking;
   Raindrops are falling and the earth is drinking.
   Raindrops keep plants green, and our crops keep growing.
   Raindrops are falling and the earth is drinking.

2. Raindrops will go back, back up where they came from.
   Raindrops will go back, back up where they came from.
   Moisture will rise up with evaporation.
   Raindrops will go back, back up where they came from.

The Rain Cycle

Children must be made aware that the same water is used over and over on the earth. The rain falls from the sky through a process called condensation, whereby vapor is turned into drops of water. After these drops of water fall to the earth and are used in various ways, the cycle is completed by the water evaporating back up into the air. The simplest way to demonstrate evaporation is to put a shallow pan of water out in the classroom and watch it disappear over a period of time. Put another shallow pan of water outside in direct sunlight and see which evaporates more quickly.

GA1522

Condensation can be demonstrated by putting heated water in a sealed container (a pop bottle or a jar with a screw-on lid). As the water cools, water droplets can be seen forming in the upper areas of the bottle.

Common Cycles

Many common cycles happen around us all of the time that we don't give much thought to. Fill in the blanks on the circles to go with the cycles illustrated.

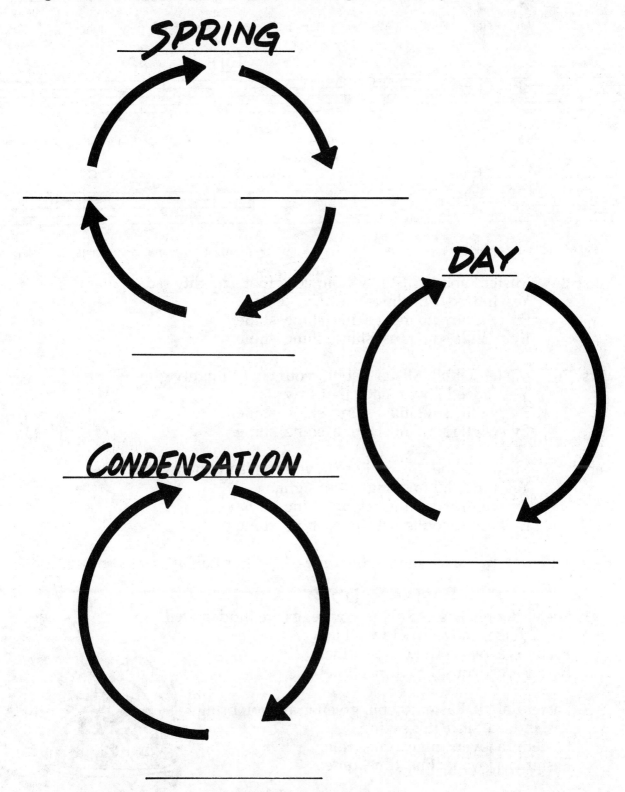

Mister Rabbit
African-American Play Song

Mi-ster Rab-bit, Mis-ter Rab-bit, Your ear's mi-ghty long! Yes, in-

deed, they're put on wrong___. Ev-ry lit-tle soul must

shine, shine, shine___, Ev-ry lit-tle soul must shine___, shine, shine.

Verse 2: Mister Rabbit, Mister Rabbit, your foot's mighty red!
Yes, indeed, I'm almost dead.
Ev'ry little soul must shine, shine, shine,
Ev'ry little soul must shine, shine, shine.

Verse 3: Mister Rabbit, Mister Rabbit, your coat's mighty gray.
Yes, indeed, 'twas made that way.
Ev'ry little soul must shine, shine, shine,
Ev'ry little soul must shine, shine, shine.

Verse 4: Mister Rabbit, Mister Rabbit, your tail's mighty white.
Yes, indeed, I'm going out of sight.
Ev'ry little soul must shine, shine, shine,
Ev'ry little soul must shine, shine, shine.

Here are four new verses sung to the tune of "Mister Rabbit":

Easter Rabbit

1. Easter Rabbit, Easter Rabbit, your eggs are hidden well.
   Yes, indeed, and where I won't tell.
   Easter is a joyous time, time, time.
   Easter is a joyous time, time, time!

2. Easter Rabbit, Easter Rabbit, green grass you bring.
   Yes, indeed, since it is spring.
   Easter is a joyous time, time, time,
   Easter is a joyous time, time, time!

GA1522

3. Easter Rabbit, Easter Rabbit, your flow'rs are so bright!
   Yes, indeed, they're a colorful sight.
   Easter is a joyous time, time, time,
   Easter is a joyous time, time, time!

4. Easter Rabbit, Easter Rabbit, your basket is lush!
   Yes, indeed, but I must rush.
   Easter is a joyous time, time, time,
   Easter is a joyous time, time, time!

The Chicken's Egg

Use the patterns of the chicken and the egg on page 124 for a fun matching game for Easter. Copy enough chickens for half of your class and enough eggs for the other half. If your class has an odd number of students, you'll need to take one of the patterns yourself to match with a student. For each pair of a chicken and an egg there is a corresponding pair of words that you will write on them. For instance, write the word *cup* on the egg and the word *saucer* on the chicken. The children will cut out whichever pattern they're given and take their patterns around the room trying to find which egg goes with which chicken and vice-versa. Use these words of things that go together and add your own pairs as well. Children may color the chickens and eggs once they've been matched. They may wish to decorate the eggs as if for Easter. A huge collage could be put up of all the chickens and their matching eggs.

Words to use for chickens:
1. saucer
2. shoe
3. chairs
4. mother
5. knife
6. sand
7. cookies
8. mashed potatoes
9. pepper
10. horse
11. light bulb
12. bolt

Words to use for eggs:
1. cup
2. sock
3. table
4. child
5. fork
6. sea
7. milk
8. gravy
9. salt
10. cart
11. socket
12. nut

Add your own ideas to this list.

GA1522

Chicken Pattern

Egg Pattern

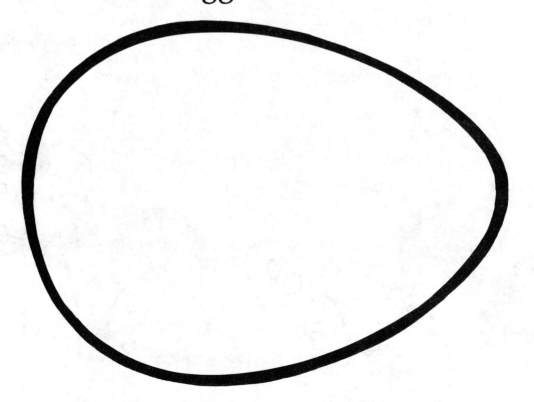

May

125

The Meadowlands
Czechoslovakian Folk Song

Walking tempo

Out to the mea-dow - lands we go, walk-ing in the sun-light,

walk-ing in the sun - light. Out to the mea-dow - lands we go, where the wa-ving fields of

bar - ley grow. Hey! Stream-lets are rush-ing by, down from the moun-tain high,

sing-ing they on-ward go, swift-ly the wa-ters flow. Stream-lets are rush-ing by,

down from the moun-tain high, sing-ing, they on-ward go, swift-ly they flow.

Verse 2:

Home from the meadowlands we go,
Strolling in the twilight, strolling in the twilight,
Home from the meadowlands we go,
Sweet the summer air in evening's glow. Hey!

Streamlets are rushing by, down from the mountain high.
Singing, they onward go; swiftly the waters flow.
Streamlets are rushing by, down from the mountain high.
Singing, they onward go; swiftly they flow.

GA1522

Here are two new verses sung to the tune of "The Meadowlands."

Travel Anywhere

1. If you could travel anywhere,
   Would it be by airplane
   Or would it be by train?
   If you could travel anywhere,
   What's your choice of transport to get there? Go!

   England or sunny Spain,
   Georgia or up to Maine,
   China or Korea,
   Denmark or Venezuela,
   West Indies, Africa, Peru, or Australia,
   Iceland or Mexico, where would you go?

2. Traveling by foot or by car,
   Notice what's around you,
   Use your eyes; take in the view.
   Traveling by foot or by car,
   Read a map to know just where you are. Go!

   Austria or Brazil, Japan or Israel,
   France or Puerto Rico or to the Belgian Congo,
   New York or Italy, Greece or the Arctic Sea,
   Who knows, it may be soon—fly to the moon!

Continental Cakewalk

Here's a fun way for children to become more familiar with the different countries of the world and the continents on which they're located. Make the game as easy or as difficult as your class can handle. On large squares of construction paper, write the names of either a country or an animal that is associated with a particular continent. Lay these pieces out on the floor in either a square or circular pattern. Also write the name of each country and animal on slips of paper and place in a box.

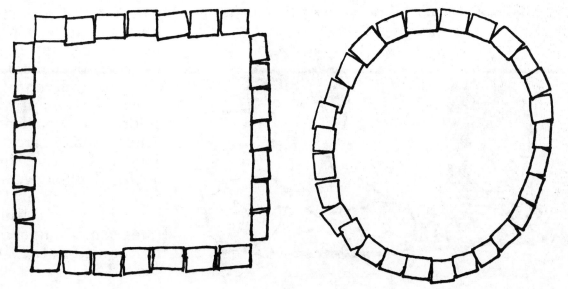

GA1522

Since this is similar to a cakewalk, you'll need music for the children to walk with. It's preferable to use music from various cultures if at all possible. To begin the cakewalk, each child stands on a square. When the music starts, children begin walking to their right around the square or circle. When the music stops, everyone must stop on a square. The teacher then randomly draws a slip of paper out of the box. Whoever is on the square that matches the paper that was drawn must tell what continent goes with that country or animal. For instance, Nigeria is in Africa; kangaroo is from Australia. Vary the game by having the children tell the capital of the country, the official language, or chief export. Tailor this game to suit what your class is studying. Reward each correct answer with some kind of small prize (a sticker, a pencil, etc.). As soon as a child has given an answer, he or she turns over the square he or she was standing on to reveal the correct answer only to himself or herself. If correct, that child reveals the answer to everyone, takes the square, gets the prize, and sits down. The teacher then puts that slip of paper into another box. If incorrect, the child turns the square back over without revealing the correct answer to anyone else. The slip of paper returns to the answer box where it may come up again, and the game continues. End the game after a set time period.

Postcards with the Most

Provide three postcards for each child to write and "send" to three friends from three different places using the patterns on page 129. On each card the children must tell at least three things about the country (which they've researched) that they're "visiting"–for instance, the capital or other cities visited, climate, language(s), food eaten that is native to that country, a historical site or point of interest visited, a famous leader of the country whom they saw. For example, a postcard from Italy could tell about visiting in Venice and taking a gondola ride; eating manicotti in Rome, the capital city; and visiting the Vatican and seeing the Pope. Each person receiving a postcard should read it aloud to the class. Then the cards could be put on display for anyone to read at free times. Each child will deliver his or her own cards after writing them by either laying them on their friends' desks or placing them in lockers or mailboxes. Three is the requirement, but encourage children to research and write as many cards as they'd like to. They might also draw and color a picture on the other side that illustrates something about the country they've "visited."

Postcard Patterns

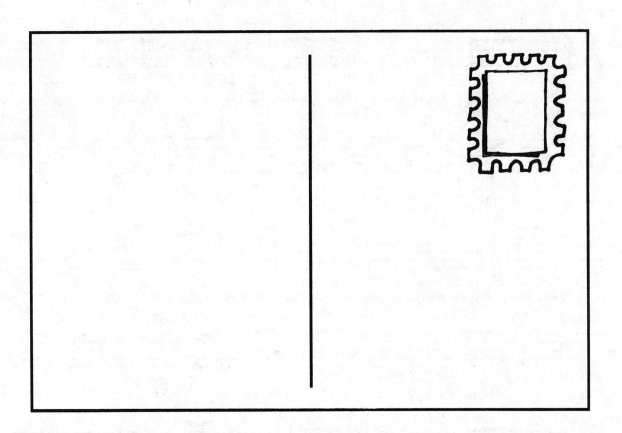

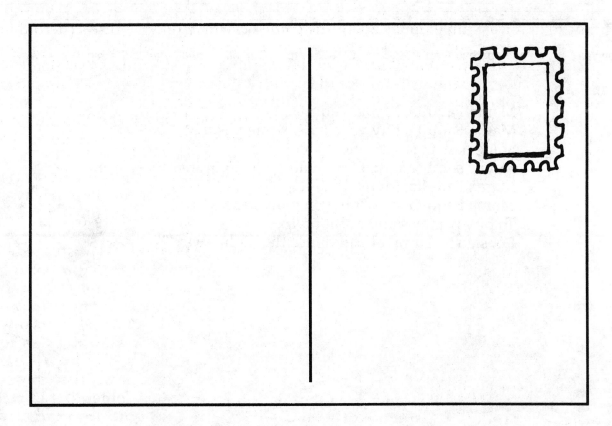

GA1522

Mama Paquita
Carnival Song from Brazil

Ma - ma Pa - qui - ta, Ma - ma Pa - qui - ta, Ma - ma Pa - qui - ta buy your ba - by a pa - pa - ya, A ripe pa - pa - ya and a ba - na - na, A ripe ba - na - na that your ba - by will en - joy. Ma - ma - ma - ma, Ma - ma Pa - qui - ta, Ma - ma Pa - qui - ta, Ma - ma Pa - qui - ta says, "I hav - en't an - y mon - ey to buy pa - payas and ripe ban - an - as, Let's go to Car - ni - val and dance the night a - way!"

Verse 2:

Mama Paquita, Mama Paquita,
Mama Paquita, buy your baby some pajamas,
Some new pajamas, and a sombrero,
A new sombrero that your baby will enjoy, ma-ma-ma-ma,
Mama Paquita, Mama Paquita,
Mama Paquita says, "I haven't any money
To buy pajamas and a sombrero,
Let's go to Carnival and dance the night away!"

GA1522

Here are two new verses sung to the tune of "Mama Paquita":

In a Rain Forest

1. In a rain forest, in a rain forest,
   In a rain forest you'll find giant plants and insects,
   Some giant insects that we must protect,
   And plants that give us cures that we need to detect.
   In a, in a, in a rain forest, in a rain forest,
   In a rain forest there are animals of all kinds,
   Like giant tree sloths and other rare finds,
   Let's save rain forests and not burn them all away!

2. In a rain forest, in a rain forest,
   In a rain forest you'll find valuable new treasures;
   And these new treasures are hard to measure
   Because all haven't been discovered yet to date.
   In a, in a, in a rain forest, in a rain forest,
   In a rain forest trees make air to keep us breathing.
   It would not be wise to ruin paradise,
   Let's save rain forests and not burn them all away!

Rain Forest Treasure Hunt

Before the students arrive for class, the teacher puts labels of things found in a rain forest all over the room. Include these on your labels:

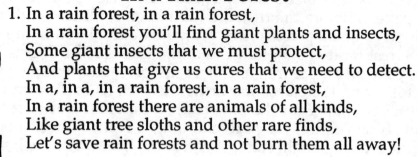

strangler fig plant
giant orchids
ferns
bamboo
beetle
army ant nest
curassow
giant tree frog
iguana lizard
fer-de-lance snake
armadillo
tamandua (lesser anteater)
tapir
sloth
saki (monkey)
tribes of natives

twisted vines
palms
mushrooms
periwinkle tree
dragonfly
parasol ant nest
cocoa trees
gecko lizard
bushmaster snake
termite mound
giant anteater
silky anteater
jaguar
peccary (wild pig)
spider monkey
stream

Add your own ideas to this list.

The labels can be taped to objects like chairs or whatever else you have in your room. In other words, your whole classroom has been converted into a rain forest by these labels.

On the treasure hunt there will be two teams. There are ten clues for each team located at various points in the rain forest. While searching for their treasures, they will make important discoveries along the way. To avoid confusion of the two teams getting each other's clues, it would be wise to put the clues on different colored papers. Before the treasure hunt begins, all ten clues for each team must be written on small pieces of colored paper and placed in the right progression at rain forest locations around the room. The teacher begins by telling the class that they are on a treasure hunt in a rain forest and that they will find their treasure by following the clues. She or he then hands each team the first clues. One clue is on blue paper for the blue team; a different clue is on red paper for the red team. For instance, the blue clue might read, "Check under the cocoa tree," while the red clue might state, "Look at the beetle." As each team progresses to the location given by the last clue, they'll discover a new clue. Since many discoveries about the rain forest have not been made yet, these are imaginary discoveries. It's possible that they could come true someday though.

Nine sample clues might be:
1. You have discovered a new anesthetic for pain! Check the termite mound next.
2. You have found a new chemical that can be used in glue. Proceed to the stream.
3. You have discovered an entirely new species of fish! Go to the ferns.
4. You have found a new type of herb which slows the aging process! Give three cheers, then head over to the giant tree frog.
5. You have discovered a new type of oil to lubricate engine parts. Go to the periwinkle tree.
6. You have found a new kind of nut that is edible. Trek on to the peccary (wild pig).
7. You have uncovered a form of rubber that never wears out. Shout "Kawabunga!" and skip over to the mushrooms.
8. You accidentally find a new spice that sweetens without being fattening! Hike to the giant orchids.
9. Congratulations! You've reached the end of your rain forest treasure hunt and have discovered an unknown orchid that leads to a cure for cancer!

Have the students keep all of their clues. Discuss all of the treasures the rain forest has to offer, and why it's important to preserve the rain forest, if for no other reason than that we don't know what we might be destroying. Discuss what other diseases might be cured by things found in the rain forest.

Variations of the treasure hunt that will make it more fun are to add silly actions on getting from one clue to the next, such as walk backwards, hop on one foot, crawl, duck walk, etc. Be creative and add your own ideas to expand the treasure hunt.

Tinga Layo
West Indies Calypso Song

Tin - ga La - yo! Come, lit - tle don-key, come; Tin-ga La - yo!

Come, lit - tle don-key, come.
1. My don-key walk, my don-key talk, my don-key
2. My don-key eat, my don-key sleep, my don-key

eat with a knife and fork; Tin-ga La - yo! Come, lit - tle don-key, come; Tin-ga
kick with his two hind feet;

La - yo! Come, lit - tle don-key, come. Come, lit - tle don-key, come—.

Here are two new verses sung to the tune of "Tinga Layo":

In the Shelter

1. In the shelter so many good pets wait,
   In the shelter so many good pets wait.
   If you want dogs, if you want cats,
   You'll have a choice since the number's vast.
   In the shelter so many good pets wait.
   In the shelter so many good pets wait.

2. In the shelter so many good pets wait,
   In the shelter so many good pets wait.
   If you choose one to call your own
   Make sure you give him a lasting home.
   In the shelter so many good pets wait.
   In the shelter so many good pets wait.

GA1522

The Housebreaking (A Finger Puppet Play)

This finger puppet play will help children learn how to overcome one of the main reasons dogs are stuck in backyards for most of their lives or returned to animal shelters shortly after being adopted: housebreaking problems. They'll have more fun putting on a short play using these finger puppets. And maybe it will lead to less lonely dogs!

Have the children color the copies of the puppets from this page, cut them out, and tape the tabs together in the back.

Children will perform this mini play behind a table with their finger puppets showing just above the tabletop. By putting a tablecloth over the table, you can hide the puppeteers and they'll be able to read their lines instead of having to memorize them.

(Puddles the Puppy is onstage all by himself looking around and whimpering. Father enters as Puddles hangs his head and whimpers louder.)

Father: (looking down beside Puddles) Oh, no! Not again! (looking offstage right) Doris, come in the living room and see what your puppy from the animal shelter has done once again!

Doris: (entering from stage right) What do you mean? (looks down) Oh, Puddles, not again! Why can't you learn not to go inside the house? Hector, come see what your puppy that you had to have so badly has done in the living room once again!

(Hector enters from stage right)

Hector: Why don't you let me train him?

Father: Do you know how?

Mother: If you can keep Puddles from ruining my carpet any more, then go right ahead!

Hector: We can use my old playpen that's out in the garage as a dog crate for Puddles. We just have to wrap it with coated wire so Puddles can't get out. We'll set it up in the laundry room where the floor can be mopped.

Father: I don't understand. What good will all this do?

Hector: Puddles will come to consider the crate as his own bed or safe area, and he won't want to soil his own home. I'll put in some toys and a little dog treat to make him feel more at home.

Mother: But when you let him out in the laundry room, won't he make a mistake on the cement floor?

Hector: At first he might, but I'll mop it up with a rag, and then I'll anchor the rag outdoors with a stone or a stake where we want Puddles to go regularly. From then on, I'll take Puddles there immediately after taking him out of the crate.

Father: How often will you have to do this?

Hector: Since he's only twelve weeks old he should go out first thing in the morning, midmorning, noon, upon waking from naps, after each meal, and at bedtime.

Mother: That often?

Hector: Well, as he gets older we can take him out in the morning, then I can take him out after school, after he eats, and before bed.

Father: Ok, I'll take Puddles out at noon and at bedtime.

Mother: And I'll take him out midmorning and when he wakes up from naps.

Hector: And remember when he goes in the right place to give him loving words, pats, and smiles. But if he makes a mistake just scowl and say, "No, no," before you hustle him outside to the right spot.

(Puddles barks twice and acts happy.)

135

Father: (looking down) Well, it looks like Puddles thinks that's a good method.
Mother: Well, if this works that leaves one problem.
(Hector, Father, and Puddles all turn and look at Mother.)
Hector: (concerned) What's that?
Mother: If it works, we're going to have to give Puddles a new name!
(Everyone laughs and Puddles barks.)

The End

Discuss with your class that animal shelters across the United States are crowded with unwanted and homeless animals, many of which must be "put to sleep" to make room for even more animals. Nearly eight million dogs and cats must be humanely destroyed each year because there aren't enough homes for them all. Get more information about this problem from your local animal shelter or Humane Society. You might take your class on a field trip to the local animal shelter or Humane Society. A major contributor to the pet overpopulation problem is that pet owners are carelessly not getting their companion animals spayed or neutered (an operation performed by a veterinarian to stop the animal from having kittens or puppies). Copy enough of the pages of the Cheshire Cat parts and the puzzle outline for each child to have one of each.

This Cheshire Cat is smiling because he knows the reasons why everyone should spay or neuter pets. Look at the parts of the Cheshire Cat and at the reasons. Cut out all the parts, and try them out on the pattern of the Cheshire Cat. If they fit, it means they're true reasons to spay or neuter your pets. Can you pick out the parts that will fit on the first try and make the wise Cheshire Cat appear? Once you've fitted the parts correctly, glue them on the puzzle. Color your wise Cheshire Cat and take him home.

Making the Wise Cheshire Cat Appear

GA1522

Cheshire Cat Puzzle Parts

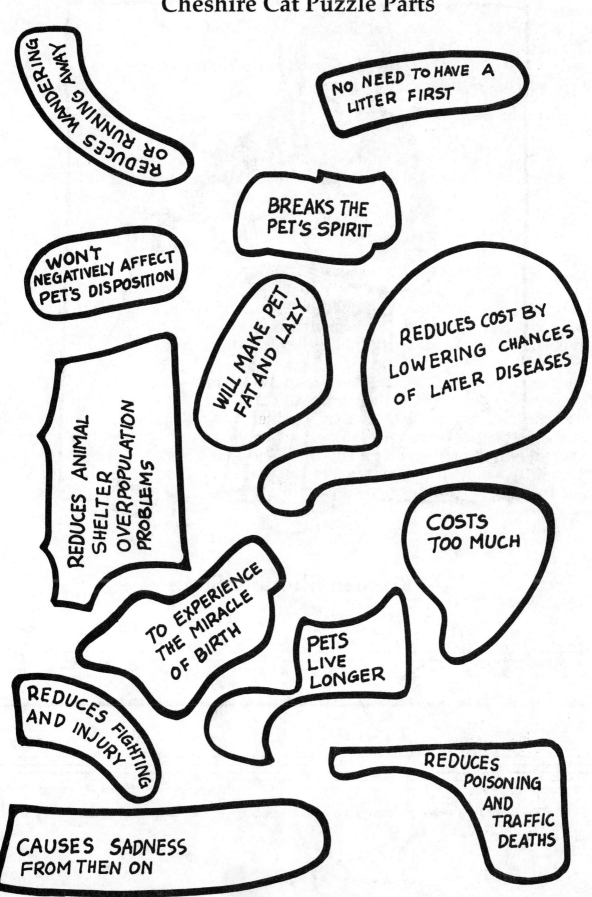

REDUCES WANDERING OR RUNNING AWAY

NO NEED TO HAVE A LITTER FIRST

BREAKS THE PET'S SPIRIT

WON'T NEGATIVELY AFFECT PET'S DISPOSITION

WILL MAKE PET FAT AND LAZY

REDUCES COST BY LOWERING CHANCES OF LATER DISEASES

REDUCES ANIMAL SHELTER OVERPOPULATION PROBLEMS

COSTS TOO MUCH

TO EXPERIENCE THE MIRACLE OF BIRTH

PETS LIVE LONGER

REDUCES FIGHTING AND INJURY

REDUCES POISONING AND TRAFFIC DEATHS

CAUSES SADNESS FROM THEN ON

Russian Slumber Song

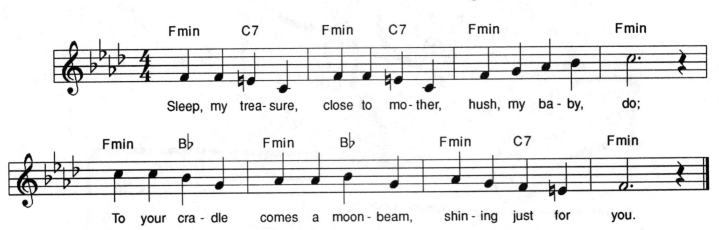

Sleep, my trea-sure, close to mo-ther, hush, my ba-by, do;

To your cra-dle comes a moon-beam, shin-ing just for you.

138

Here are two new verses sung to the tune of "Russian Slumber Song":

Memorial Day

1. There's a day that comes in May to recall those who've gone,
   Loved ones who were dear to us within our hearts live on.

2. Celebrate and decorate on Memorial Day.
   We'll remember all our loved ones who have passed away.

Memorial Day Rebuses

(Answer key for the teacher's eyes only: 1. Flowers, 2. Picnic, 3. Veterans, 4. Cemetery, 5. Family, 6. Decoration)

Copy for the students.

These rebuses name six words associated with Memorial Day. Can you guess what they are? To solve a rebus, guess what each object is and spell it. Then add or subtract the letters.

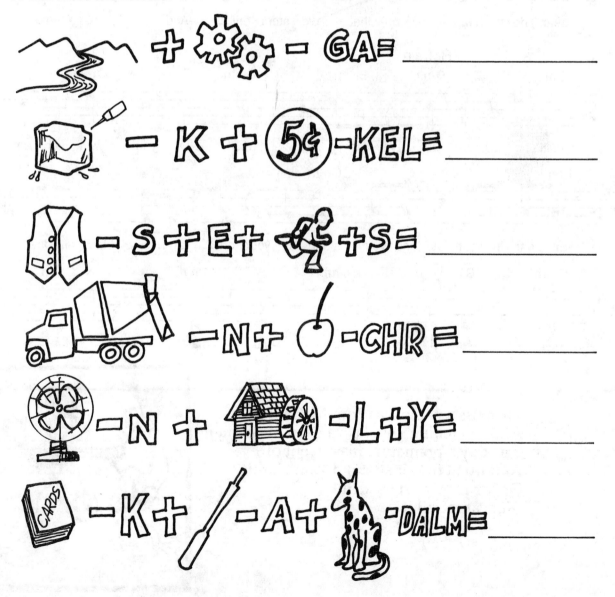

139

Drill, Ye Tarriers
Irish-American Folk Song

Cmin — With Gusto — Cmin — Cmin
Ev - ry mor - nin' 'round sev-en o'-clock— there are four and twen-ty men a—

G7 — Cmin — Cmin
drill-in' on the rock, and the boss comes 'round— and he says, "Keep still,— and—

Cmin — G7 — Cmin — G7
bear down hea - vy on that old steel drill—. And drill, ye tar - ri - ers,

Refrain

Cmin — Cmin — Bb — Cmin — Cmin
drill!" Drill, ye tar - ri - ers, drill! Oh, you work all day for

Fmin — Cmin — G7
su - gar in your tay, and you stand by your drill— and— blast all day—. Oh,

Cmin — G7 — Cmin — Cmin — Cmin
drill, ye tar - ri - ers, drill! And blast and fire!

Verse 2:

The boss's name was Tom McCann,
And I'm telling you, he's a darn mean man!
One day a premature blast went off,
And up in the air shot old Tom Goth!
Oh, drill, ye tarriers, drill!
(Repeat refrain.)

140

GA1522

Verse 3:   When next payday came around,
            Tom Goth a dollar short was found.
            When he asked, "What for?" came this reply,
            "You were docked for time you were up in the sky!"
            So, drill, ye tarriers, drill!
            Refrain

Here are two new verses sung to the tune of "Drill, Ye Tarriers":

School is Practic'ly Done

1. Ev'ry mornin' at 7:00 o'clock,
   My alarm clock rings and wakes me up with a shock!
   Then my mom comes up and knocks on my door,
   And she says, "Get up, you've got a few days more,
   "But school is practic'ly done!"

Refrain: School is practic'ly done!
            Gotta work today and learn what all you may;
            Then when summer comes you'll have free time to play.
            Yes, school is practic'ly done! It's almost out!

2. When I'm thinkin' I just can't go on
   I look up at the clock and half the day is gone!
   And the teacher says, "It's time to eat lunch.
   Put your books away and make a line. Don't bunch!
   Yes, school is practic'ly done!
   Refrain

3. The afternoon goes by pretty darn fast,
   And I see it's already time to go home at last.
   And my best friend says, "Let's go play some ball."
   And I know that I will have to heed his call.
   And school is practic'ly done!
   Refrain

Sweet Dreams of the School Year Gone By

Have each student bring an old pillowcase from home for all of the class and teachers to sign. Use permanent markers. Then when the children take them home and sleep on them, they'll have sweet dreams of the school year gone by!

Begin with the End

Near the last day of school, have your students think back over the year about what they liked that they did in your class. Then have each student write a short note to someone who will be in your class next year. Students won't know who they're writing to, so they should just tell some things they liked about being in your class or about you and keep it general. Then you will collect their notes, read them to evaluate your own year's activities and lessons, and save them over the summer. At the beginning of the next school year, you'll hand the notes out to your new class and say that your students from last year wanted to leave you a personal note about what it's like to be in this class. This should get the new school year off to a very positive start! And it will also give you a chance to evaluate what you did and maybe change things to make the next school year even better!